4

*f*P

ALSO BY NORMAN FISCHER

BOOKS

Opening to You: Zen-Inspired Translations of the Psalms
Taking Our Places: The Buddhist Path to Truly Growing Up

POETRY COLLECTIONS

Precisely the Point Being Made
Success
Slowly but Dearly
I Was Blown Back

for Edie,

SAILING HOME

The journey home

Using the Wisdom of Homer's *Odyssey*
to Navigate Life's Perils and Pitfalls

grows warmer + warmer.

Yours

NORMAN FISCHER

Norman

FREE PRESS

New York London Toronto Sydney

B'ham   *7.3.08*

FREE PRESS

A Division of Simon & Schuster, Inc.

1230 Avenue of the Americas

New York, NY 10020

First Free Press hardcover edition June 2008

FREE PRESS and colophon are trademarks of
Simon & Schuster, Inc.

For information about special discounts for bulk
purchases, please contact Simon & Schuster Special Sales
at 1-800-456-6798 or business@simonandschuster.com

Book design by Ellen R. Sasahara

Manufactured in the United States of America

1   3   5   7   9   10   8   6   4   2

Library of Congress Cataloging-in-Publication Data
Fischer, Norman.
Sailing home : using the wisdom of Homer's Odyssey to
navigate life's perils and pitfalls / Norman Fischer.
p. cm.
1. Religious life—Zen Buddhism. I. Title.
BQ9286.F57 2008
294.3'444—dc22
2007052352
ISBN-13: 978-1-4165-6021-0
ISBN-10:   1-4165-6021-1

This book is dedicated to the practitioners of the Everyday Zen Foundation, good friends all, from the San Francisco Bay area, the Pacific Northwest, and Chacala, Mexico, who responded so enthusiastically to the talks on which it is based. For that, and for many years of warm side-by-side spiritual practice, I will always be grateful.

Contents

It is as though the ability to comprehend experience through metaphor were a sense, like seeing or touching or hearing, with metaphors providing the only ways to perceive and experience much of the world. Metaphor is as much a part of our functioning as our sense of touch, and as precious.

George Lakoff and Mark Johnson, *Metaphors We Live By*[1]

I keep trying to return
Nothing makes too much sense
but in various ways

Steve Benson, in *Open Clothes*[2]

Acknowledgments

It took a long time to write this simple book, and I needed help and encouragement. Michael Friedman transcribed, with love, the initial talks at Green Gulch Zen temple in which I first began using the tales of *The Odyssey* as metaphors for the spiritual journey. Students at the Everyday Zen Dharma Seminar heard the material again, and added their own ideas to what I had worked out. I ruminated still more at talks in retreats in the Pacific Northwest and in Mexico. Marc Lesser studied my notes and made suggestions. Novelist Ruth Ozeki read the manuscript and made invaluable professional comments. Poet Steve Benson also read an early draft of the manuscript and added valuable insights. My friend and literary agent Michael Katz spent a lot of time working through the original idea for the book with me, and was succeeded by Lindsay Edgecombe from Levine Greenberg, who was on the ball every minute. Sasha Raskin expertly took care of the pesky permissions. Working with Leslie Meredith and her colleagues at Free Press has been easy and pleasant. They are hardworking professionals in a tough business. Without the many volunteers who make Everyday Zen go (especially Tim Burnett, the resident priest at the Red Cedar Zen Community in Bellingham, Washington, who built the original Web site) I would never have been able even to dream of a project like this. May it, for their sake, be of benefit to others.

SAILING HOME

Introduction

WHENEVER I GO TO A Zen meditation retreat, sooner or later—by the third or fourth day if not the first or second—I get the classic feeling of déjà vu: *Haven't I lived this moment before?* I sit on my meditation cushion, in my Buddhist robes, delivering a formal Zen discourse. I look out at my silent, dignified listeners. *Haven't I given this talk before?—and to these same people? Possibly many times?* And what day, what year, what place *is* this anyway? Strangely timeless, the déjà vu moment seems very real to me, though it is utterly different from the normal pressured moments of busy clock time that mark the purposeful hours and days of my ordinary life.

I have been a Zen Buddhist student, priest, or teacher for most of my life and have done countless Zen retreats. No wonder I have the feeling I've been here before! Getting older might be a factor, too: I've been going along in this body for many decades, through many subtle changes of aging, getting up, sitting down, eating meals, going to the toilet, walking, standing, laughing, crying, wondering about the nature of sensation, being, and time, writing books and poems, spring, summer, fall, winter, year after year, people dying, new people being born, the daily news always different and the same: perhaps the déjà vu experience becomes more normal the longer you live. Maybe déjà vu is just the ordinary, actual feeling of *being in time,* an astonishing experience, though we're so used to it we don't much pay attention.

Another thing about the déjà vu moment: it doesn't seem to arrive out of the blue; it feels as if it has been here all along, lurking in the background of my living but only rising into consciousness now and then. Most of the time I am too busy for it, so mesmerized and absorbed by the convincing details and dramas of life that there's no room for it. It seems to take something radical—such as a Zen retreat, a whack on the head, or a sudden shock of some sort—to bring forth the moment into awareness. I may have become a Zen Buddhist priest so that I could frequent meditation retreats where I'd be bound to bump into this uncanny, rare moment, which is at the same time utterly common and ordinary—I would be experiencing it quite often if only I were paying more attention. What a ridiculous predicament! At my talks during meditation retreats I share this ridiculous predicament with my fellow meditators, who, like me, are also gloriously, luminously, and constantly stuck in the déjà vu moment, but have also forgotten to notice it, and are aware that they are missing something important, fundamental, and beautiful about their lives. Like me, they also feel the need to make an earnest effort to return home to this moment, even though they've never actually left it.

The mystery (and pain!) of our lives is that we are where we need to be, but we don't know it. The spiritual odyssey, life's deepest and most significant undertaking, involves great effort. It leads us on through many disasters and troubles in the inevitably checkered course of our living and growing, and in the end brings us back where we started from, to ourselves, only now with a more seasoned appreciation. There's an old Zen saying: "Before I began Zen practice, mountains were mountains and rivers were rivers. Entering Zen practice, I saw that mountains were not mountains and rivers were not rivers. Now again, after long effort, I see that mountains are mountains and rivers are rivers." The spiritual odyssey is full of déjà vu experiences, full of irony, depth, strangeness, and wonder. Full of paradox. In it, everything changes and nothing changes. And we will all make this journey, each in our own way, no matter how much we insist on ignoring, denying, forgetting, or working against it.

In a story from the Jewish tradition, which is also told in the Muslim tradition, and many others, a poor tailor from the shtetl has a dream that a treasure is buried underneath a bridge leading to a castle. The tailor packs his bags and journeys to the capital city. He approaches the bridge he saw in his dream, but there is a Cossack standing guard. For long hours the tailor stands gazing at the bridge, not knowing what to do. Finally the Cossack asks him why he has been standing there so long and the innocent and honest tailor tells him the story. The Cossack laughs uproariously. "Foolish Jew," he says, "believing the fantasies of sleep. Let me tell you the difference between you and me. I too have had a dream. I dreamt that under the stove of a Jewish tailor in the shtetl was buried a treasure. You travel all this way at such cost of time and effort chasing dreams for nothing. I, on the other hand, know a dream for a dream and don't waste my time." The tailor promptly went home, dug under his stove, found the treasure, and lived out the rest of his days a prosperous man.

We are all born with a dream. It wants to lead us on, elsewhere, in search of our heart's desire. Maybe we are practical, down-to-earth people like the Cossack. We ignore the dream and decide to live our life stuck where we are, in a world we take to be real but in fact have manufactured, without knowing we've manufactured it, paying no attention to the vastness of our lives, the uncanny weird mysteries that may be presenting themselves to us at every turn, only we are too busy and too prejudiced to notice.

Or maybe we are better dreamers than this. We do follow the dream, but fail to see its true import, and so are inevitably disappointed when it doesn't pan out as we had expected. So we dust ourselves off and follow the next dream that comes along, and then the next and the next, always dissatisfied, always seeking something we never seem to find.

Or maybe we are like the simple tailor in the story. We follow our dream. And we pay close enough attention to what happens in the process to recognize (with a little help from a Cossack!)

that what we are seeking has been there right under our stoves all along, only we hadn't noticed it before. So we go home and dig a little.

I have seen just this sort of thing happen many times. I lived for many years in Zen centers. People would often come to visit these centers, with a great longing and envy, imagining that spiritual fulfillment was to be found inside the temple compound, a place where they could not possibly remain. They would come for a year or a week or a day, longing, even as they were there, to be there more frequently, and for longer stays. And then, if they were lucky, eventually they would realize what was obvious to me all along (though it never did any good to tell them because they would not listen): that the spiritual key they were looking for was to be found right where they were, in their work or family life, on the meditation cushion that was right in their own home, in the living room next to the easy chair. As Zen Master Dogen writes, "Why give up the seat in your own house and wander uselessly in the dust of remote lands?"

The story about the tailor turns on the traditional Jewish concept of *teshuvah*, return. Teshuvah is the spiritual effort we must constantly make to come back to the depth and truth of our living, from which we are constantly straying simply because we are normal human beings living in a normal, distracting, human world. Fall and redemption, in other words, didn't only happen long ago to the characters in the Bible: they are happening all the time in us as well. Although the Jewish sacred calendar sets aside special times of the year for teshuvah (the High Holidays of Yom Kippur and Rosh Hashanah), the deeper sense is that teshuvah—this leaving and having to return again and again—is the constant shape of human consciousness.

Return is also a fact of nature: the universe expands and contracts, the tides go out and come in, celestial bodies go around and around, the seasons begin, endure, draw to a close, come around again. The spiritual journey, the human journey, is as natural as this. We begin at home, we leave home, we return home. Even when it looks like we're going far afield, we're always on our way back. We have what we need, and we are where we are going; the spiritual journey is a journey of return.

How do we make this journey? There are no maps. The path is mysterious, dark. It leads us to the corners, the subtexts, of our lives, the in-between, unconscious, unknowable places. We think we know who we are and what our lives are about. But suppose we don't. Suppose our lives are not what we think they are; suppose something else is going on, deep streams flowing underground that come to the surface only now and again, in little springs or freshets or maybe only in telltale spots of moisture where weeds or scraggly flowers grow. And suppose that the task of our lives is not so much to shape or control our stories so that they will turn out according to our preference or preconception but rather to recognize that our stories, the visible images of our lives, are cover stories, narratives that hide within them deeper, underground narratives, that we can sense and taste now and again but never fully comprehend.

This is the territory of religion and myth, the province of spiritual practice. And yes, there are traditions, protocols, studies, useful spiritual activities we can engage in. We can practice meditation, prayer, or some other form of spiritual exercise with discipline and commitment; we can study, imagine, write in a journal, make art. We can become part of a spiritual community, and we can show up to practice side by side with people of that community, helping to take responsibility for it. We can seek mentors, teachers, or spiritual directors, and we can work with them sensitively, receiving their guidance with appreciation, but never without taking responsibility for our own development. And we can follow a teaching of some sort, whether it is the religion we were brought up in and have long been familiar with, or some other religion, or combination of religions, or no religion at all but some more secular form of spiritual wisdom.

Yes, we can and ought to do some or all these things. They will make a big difference. This book, in fact, is one such spiritual aid; it will help you to appreciate the shape and feeling for the journey, will give you tools and reflections to keep you company, and perhaps also steady your step as you walk forward into the darkness. But no book, no practice, no community, no scripture can ensure that things will turn out as you want them to—nor, even, that you can be sure, at any point, of where you are or where you are going. For the spiritual odyssey is more mysterious than any teaching, community, or mentor can explain (though there is no shortage of explanations). And because the journey takes us in the end back to the beginning, back home where we started from, it is an odd journey, a heartfelt journey, a sentimental journey, a journey of déjà vu.

In Zen Buddhism the spiritual process is imagined as a domestic art, the training of an ox. The Zen Oxherding pictures show a lonely young person leaving the busy world in search of the ox, an ordinary water buffalo, most common of all farm animals. The ox represents the mind or heart. The youth finds the ox, settles it, tames it, rides it, and disappears. In the end he returns to the marketplace, older now, an ordinary person willing simply to help out in this world.

In Western literature the spiritual process is more likely to be envisioned as a quest. The hero sets forth from home in search of something he must find, capture, and bring back (in most traditional tales the hero is imagined as a male). He undergoes many trials and tribulations, faces implacable enemies, seeks and receives help of all sorts, confronts dangers, finally reaches his goal, and, overcoming all the odds, prevails.

Life as an arduous journey is an ancient metaphor. The Greek word *metapherein,* from which our English *metaphor* comes, is made up of the words *meta,* meaning "over, or across," implying a change of state or location, and *pherein,* meaning "to bear, or carry." In modern as in ancient Greek, the word *metapherein* commonly means "to transport, or transfer." Though we think of metaphor as a mere figure of speech, something poetic and decorative, in fact metaphors abound in our lives, underlying many concepts that we take for granted. And metaphors condition, far more than we realize, the way we think about ourselves and our world, and therefore the way we are and act. So to consider a metaphor seriously, bringing it to consciousness, turning it over in our minds and hearts, is to allow ourselves to be carried across toward some subtle yet profound inner change.

Metaphors can engage our imagination and spirit, transporting us beyond the literality of what seems to be in front of us toward what's deeper, more lively, and dynamic. Objects in the world can be defined, measured, and manipulated according to our specifications. But the heart can't be. Its requirements are more subtle, more vague. Metaphors are inexact and suggestive; they take an image or a concept and map it onto another image or concept that may seem quite disparate, as if to say "this is like that; understand this and you will understand that." In this way metaphor can help us to feel our way into the unspeakable, unchartable aspects of our lives. Seeing your life as a "spiritual odyssey" is a metaphorical truth. Contemplating your life as a spiritual odyssey can help you to enter hidden parts of your life.

This spiritual process is neither rational nor scientific; it does involve conscious effort on your part, and there may be some intelligible signposts along the way to give you a clue about where you are going. But the journey is essentially unconscious, subtle, unknowable, and surprising. This is why metaphors are necessary, and why spiritual and literary traditions are so full of them. In this book we will follow the thread of one of the greatest of all metaphors, the Odyssean journey home to Ithaca, to see what guidance it can offer as we grope our way forward toward our own spiritual destiny and fulfillment.

Some years ago I was leading a meditation retreat at Green Gulch Farm Zen Center in Muir Beach, California, where I was serving as abbot. During my daily talks I was speaking about the Buddha's great spiritual quest. I had discussed this story many times, and I was looking for a new way of making clear to my listeners that the Buddha's story is not only the historical narrative of a great religious founder but is most saliently the biography of us all. Although people understood my point intellectually, and even to some extent emotionally, it was difficult for them to identify with the Buddha. After all, the Buddha was a renunciate religious hero who had walked away from his worldly life to seek his spiritual fortune, whereas many of the people sitting the retreat with me were living normal lives in the world, with no plans to abandon those lives. They were familiar with the Buddha's story and appreciative of it, but could only see themselves outside it.

Around that time I had been, to my great delight, rereading *The Odyssey*. It struck me that Homer's tales of Odysseus were not only colorful, foundational myths of ancient Greek and therefore of Western culture; they were also spiritual teachings, metaphors of the inner life. It occurred to me that since these tales are so encoded in the Western mind, they might be clearer, more personal and straightforward for us than the Buddha's story. Odysseus is, after all, like most of us, a householder. Like us, he loves his home and his family above all. Yet, like every working man and woman, he can't remain at home; he must go forth to do battle with the world. Only then has he earned the right to return.

But to go out and come back isn't so easy. Going out takes its toll, and coming back is a struggle involving many hardships and trials. With courage, guile, and strength, with love and loyalty, Odysseus finally does return. His tale includes much of the stuff that we experience, and that the Buddha gave up: intimate relationships, passionate emotions, worldly skills and worldly goods, enemies, ambiguous and deceptive words and deeds. So in my talks that year (and for some years afterward) about the spiritual path, I began inserting stories from *The Odyssey*. Many students responded to the metaphor of leaving and returning home, and the more I read and reread *The Odyssey,* the deeper and more suggestive its details became. *The Odyssey's* metaphors helped me and my students to understand the Buddhist path, and our own progress on it, in ways we had not considered before.

The word *odyssey* is commonly taken to mean journey. But, as I've said, an odyssey is not just any journey, it is a journey of return. Homer's tale is of Odysseus' wanderings homeward after long years away fighting at Troy. The Odysseus of *The Odyssey* is not a brilliant hero on a quest, journeying forth in search of victory, glory, fame and fortune, blessings, or the truth. He's been through that already. Though reluctant, he went as a young man to fight at Troy. It was difficult. He did well. But that was long ago. Now, without a grand army or a high purpose, and with no dreams of honor, conquest, or greatness, he is struggling to return to his wife Penelope and to Ithaca, the home he left twenty years before.

Odysseus' journey home is not without its hair-raising escapes and disastrous reversals. This is not because Odysseus is a thrill-seeker or a risk-taker. With all his heart he wants to come home, and all that befalls him is simply the unavoidable consequence of that desire. Many of the worst things that happen to him are the result of his own foolishness or passion. Once or twice, just at the point of return (even within sight of the Ithacan shore!), Odysseus does or says something so stupid and so consequential that the blowback of his words or deeds sends him off again far out to sea, prolonging the agony and the longing. Yet Odysseus is no fool, nor is he without resources. Though no longer young, he is still strong and courageous. But now instead of sword and spear he relies on emotional and mental skills as his weapons: improvisation, tale-telling, guile, charm. His powerful forbearance, his undying loyalty, and his ability to hold his emotion in check sometimes also stand him in good stead. Above all, he has an unerring focus on his goal. (True, he is now and then overcome by despair or distraction, and weeps bitter tears, unable to go on, but he always comes back to his senses, and resumes the struggle.)

All this may sound familiar. *The Odyssey* has remained alive for us these thousands of years because its metaphors are so astonishingly true to life. We are Odysseus. Having made mighty efforts in our youthful days of bright hope, we eventually become tired out to the point of becoming realistic about our prospects. We realize we are not heroes. Yet we must go on with the journey, see it through until the end, even if, from time to time, we have to stop by the side of the road and weep. Why go on? Because love and loyalty require it. Besides, the emotional pull of home is compelling, no matter what we may think of it. We've got to get home. It seems as if there are no other options.

And all this may be just as true of our epoch as it is of any one of us. Perhaps we are living in a post-heroic age. Maybe the human race, so full of promise, bright ideas, and hubris, is finally weary of the toxic idealisms and thoughtless excesses of power that have been so destructive and so exhausting for so long. We have seen and done too much, and it has left us dazed and confused. Maybe, like Odysseus, we are finally ready simply to return home to what we are, to our beauty and strength as well as our limitations. Maybe we are ready to see that what's wanted and needed is what was there all along, our animal life, our love and our presence. Maybe we're ready finally to become the creatures that our deepest stories and metaphors have always described: half heavenly, half stupidly earthbound, full of wonder and awe, powerful and vulnerable. Maybe the point of our life's journey, our spiritual odyssey, is not conquest or perfection, whether spiritual or worldly, but rather the simple transformation into what we have been all along: flesh-and-blood people in a flesh-and-blood world, feeling what people feel and doing what people do. Returning home to what we are.

Could this be enough?

Part One

Setting Forth

Cutting through distraction and avoidance to begin the story

"And the sun set, and all the journeying ways were darkened."

—*The Odyssey*[1]

1 / The Sea of Stories

Our lives are full of stories, inundated by them. The day begins with the drama of the morning news and continues with stories we hear from friends, family members, coworkers, acquaintances. Popular songs regale us with stories, as do the movies, the Internet, the newspaper. Almost all our institutions, from business to psychotherapy, from school to pulpit, organize their messages through story. And at night we fall asleep to tales told in books, magazines, or television, and even our dreams weave our souls into the spell of story.

You'd think we would tire of stories, that we'd have heard it all by now. But our appetite for them is unabated. Creating, processing, and interpreting stories is a major industry, and at any given moment there are literally millions of people working on the creation of new stories that we will consume, discuss, fret about, dote over, forget, and remember.

This human obsession with stories is as old as language. Long before the printing press, or even the written word, people told stories, in verse or in song; they were blurted out loud during walking or working, whispered at night, declaimed from the holy places. People remembered and invented stories, sacred stories, profane stories, jokes, parables, fairy tales. From childhood we gravitate toward the good story and its endless fascination: "Tell it again!" children have always cried. Probably now more than ever we have access to stories from all cultures, all times, more stories every day than we could possibly absorb or pay attention to.

If you listen to stories closely, critically, and long enough, you begin to discern patterns. Boy meets girl, loses girl, gets girl back. Pride leads to a fall. Within happiness lurks the seed of tragedy. Power corrupts. The world wears down a noble character. Love suffocates, we need to break free. A hero overcomes an evil adversary. In all stories there's conflict or pressure, tension that builds to a release. Action rises, crests, then falls. Stories end happily, sadly, or with open-ended questions. I suppose you could make a list of ten or twenty or fifty plot categories into which almost all stories would fit. You could create diagrams that would chart the action of almost any story. A Russian folklorist named Vladimir Propp once did an exhaustive survey of fairy tales and folk stories in European cultures and was able to do just this. As Propp and others after him discovered, stories have deep structures with predictable variations, which is probably why they are so satisfying, even if we have heard them a thousand times. Like children, we want to hear again what we have heard before, for reassurance, because every story has a beginning and an end, a satisfying and predictable order. Stories reflect our hopes, our dreams, our fears. Just as we don't tire of looking at ourselves in the mirror, though we can be reasonably sure of what we are going to see, we never tire of stories no matter how repetitive they may be. Through stories we can experience our lives experimentally, without consequences. Through them we can safely share the common human drama, of which our own life is but a small reflective sliver.

But stories can also be enormous distractions. Immersed in the latest soap opera on television, the newspaper, the tabloids, or in the lives of our friends, we can avoid tending to what is real in our own experience, to the truth or the challenge of our living, or to the real horrors and joys of the world.

Many centuries ago the Buddha noticed with compelling acuity the way in which absorption in stories—even in our own personal stories—could, and usually did, function as an avoidance mechanism, to disastrous effect. Immersed in the passion of the tale, we forget who and what we really are, and, heedless of our patterns of thought and behavior, we go on suffering driven and unexamined lives, hurting ourselves and others in the process. This is why the Buddha devised the doctrine of "Nonself," by which he meant not that the self did not exist, but that the self depicted in stories, in gossip and myth, and in our own repeating emotional tape loops, is not a true self. Every story, by hooking us to its plotline and shaping us through its narrative structure, says far too much that is not true, and far too little that is.

As an antidote to the human obsession with stories, the Buddha taught moment-by-moment attention to the elements of perceptual, emotional, and intellectual experience. He once said, "In the seen let there be only the seen; in the heard only the heard." In other words, let go of the story and pay attention to the actual facts of your life. When you pay attention to these facts, the Buddha felt, without being swept away by the exciting plotline of your story, you will be able to see what kinds of thoughts and deeds lead to suffering and trouble, and what kinds of thoughts and deeds lead to happiness. Seeing clearly, you will choose what's happy over what's not happy, and your life and the lives of those around you will improve.

As a follower of the Buddha's teaching, I have trained myself over the years to live my life in this way, paying less attention to my story, and more attention to the fleeting moments that come and go with a tremendous fullness of emotion and perception. Being less subject to the heights and depths of my story, and more aware and tolerant of the patterns of my thinking and feeling, I think I am a happier, more balanced person.

And yet, there's no denying stories, one's own or anyone else's. To be human is to tell your tale and listen to someone else's. But it would make a difference to know that stories are stories. They are real, but not in the way we think they are when we take them too earnestly and allow them to mesmerize us. Stories are true as stories but not true as life. They require interpretation and reflection if we are to draw lessons from them. Stories teach us through their shapes, sounds, structures, and suggestions, their between-the-lines content that speaks to us through our souls rather than our minds or even our hearts.

To know that my story is not exactly mine, but is rather a wave rising up within the sea of stories, is to appreciate my story and everyone else's in a new, wider, and more significant way. Maybe by looking at stories this way we can see them as large and mysterious. Then perhaps we won't need to cling any longer to one particular version of our story as the only true story, the story of victimization or trivialization or despair or boredom; instead we might begin to see our many stories as stories of humanness, of being-aliveness, not just our own small possessions. And then, perhaps, we can be inspired by our own stories, and begin to make use of them in a new way.

Imagine: Go back in your memory to the first vivid event of your childhood that comes to mind. Maybe it's something you saw or heard, a snatch of image, a fragrance, a taste. Maybe an expanse of green grass you played on, the way it smelled and stretched out under the sun. Maybe the taste of your first birthday cake. Remember the feeling of that moment; how the place seemed, the people, the furniture, the weather. Ground yourself for a moment in the physicality of this memory. Let yourself be in it with a relaxed, curious attitude.

Now set aside this moment and begin to tell yourself the story of your life. But don't tell it résumé-style, with the usual distancing facts, where you went to school, what you accomplished, whom you married, dates of your children's births, and so on. Tell it instead as if it were a myth, the untold, hidden tale of what really occurred, the half-remembered, seemingly insignificant things, moments when you were startled suddenly out of your ordinary stupor and felt a more robust significance. Chart your life path from one such moment to the next, choosing a few moments from childhood, a few from adolescence, a few from young adulthood, and beyond. Take time to do this.

Now connect the moments one to another so that you can begin to see the narrative thread that holds them together. You could even, possibly, write all this down. Or tell it to an intimate friend. And then, when you are finished, you could do it again, with a completely different set of moments. And again and again, probably, if you wanted to. And each of the stories would be true. Each would be the story of your life. And each would feel as if it were the story also of others' lives.

Try this now, if you can. It will give you a different feeling about your life. "Who do you think you are?" will become a much more interesting question.

Thinking about *The Odyssey* in my talks at meditation retreats made me appreciate the possibility that stories, if we receive them in the right way, can heal us. Contemplating the old story of Odysseus' wanderings, experiencing it as the profound metaphor that it is, gave my listeners and me an expanded, more emotional sense of our own peregrinations, our own attempts at making the odyssey of return. Odysseus wasn't exactly the hero we had previously taken him to be, when we read Homer's poem years before. In fact, Odysseus was a lot more like us than we had remembered—sometimes a hero, yes, but just as often a fool, a hothead, a lover, a father, a friend. The opening lines of the poem set forth the basic aspects of his character:

Sing to me of the man, Muse, the man of twists and turns
driven time and again off course, once he had plundered
the hallowed heights of Troy.
Many cities of men he saw and learned their minds,
many pains he suffered, heartsick on the open sea,
fighting to save his life and bring his comrades home.[1]

Odysseus is not a simple man. Buffeted about by time and fate, he has endured much, has been thwarted time and again by forces beyond his control. In his travels—many of which he did not choose, they were chosen for him, often against his will—he has encountered and observed many sorts of people, and has learned to make use of their ways to further his own aims when he could. He has few illusions, for he has known hardship, despair, and suffering. A leathery, shifty fellow, Odysseus is a character actor more than a leading man. He is a survivor. He can be brutal when he is cornered, and he is just as willing as the next man to plunder and pillage, as he did at Troy. But he is at the same time deeply loyal, enduringly true to his wife Penelope and to Ithaca, his native land. He is a great talker, a storyteller whose tales, most of them false, are always persuasive. He is also a master of disguise who can appear as a beggar or a mighty warrior, depending on the situation. From time to time he succumbs to his passions, or even to his world-weariness. Often at crucial moments he does exactly the wrong thing, compounding his problems.

The Greek phrase rendered here as "a man of twists and turns" suggests that Odysseus' chief character trait is his wiliness. He is above all clever, deceptive, and persuasive. In ancient Greek culture this sort of quick-witted, strategic trickiness was much prized. Thanks to their intellects, more than to their strength and courage, innovative entrepreneurial people were able to craft and shape reality in order to win victories and advance societies. Athena, the goddess of wisdom who also invented many domestic arts, as well as music, appears frequently in *The Odyssey* as Odysseus' most important protector. She is also described as cunning and clever. And yet, prized and admired as these traits are, they are also understood to be problematic, for trickiness and cunning are just as likely to bring us trouble as to get us out of it. This double-edged aspect of Odysseus' character figures strongly in his story, just as it does in ours. We, too, in order for us to become persons capable of surviving and thriving in this tricky world, have to be wily and cunning. If we are too innocent, too naïve, we'll be destroyed. So we have to become pleasing people—people who can shift and change shape as conditions warrant. But our cunning and trickery have their downside, for the worldliness we develop to ensure our outer successes eventually becomes embedded in the identities that we craft for ourselves to get through this dangerous world. We begin to believe our own deceptions, and slowly drift away from our truer, more vulnerable, less presentable inner selves. This may be fine at first, but as time goes on it becomes untenable, until one day, like Odysseus, we too find ourselves "heart-sick on the open sea."

The ten-year war at Troy finally ended, Odysseus is now determined to return home to Ithaca, where his wife, Penelope, and son, Telemachus, await him. But ten years is a long time to be away, and in Odysseus' absence things on Ithaca have deteriorated. Sure that Odysseus must be dead by now, suitors vying for Penelope's hand in marriage occupy his household. Their profligate, disorganized ways (they spend days and weeks feasting, drinking up Odysseus' storehouses of wine, slaughtering his cattle) threaten to destroy Odysseus' home and substance.

The suitors represent life's blind and relentless tendency toward disorder and entropy. They are all desire, appetite—sheer, thoughtless, comfort-seeking. Absence from home is dangerous: while we are away things fall apart. When we don't pay attention to our inner life, it naturally, gradually, devolves into chaos and confusion. Someone moves in and slaughters our cattle, drinks up our wine, and dissipates the spiritual treasures we were born with and possessed as children. Without maintenance, a house falls down; without weeding, the fields go wild; and without tending, our inner lives will slowly but surely become disordered, so that when we need them most, when the circumstances of our mature lives require them, our moral fiber, our wisdom, our compassion, and our love are no longer there for us.

The situation on Ithaca in Odysseus' absence is dire. Though things seem normal enough (as they may seem in our lives), and though no one is particularly noticing (as is also the case with us), disaster is brewing.

The Odyssey's prequel, The Iliad, is a poem of going forth, a poem of honor, glory, conquest. In it, Odysseus and his comrades, led by Agamemnon and Achilles, set out for Troy to avenge the abduction of Helen, defeat the Trojans, and prove their valor. The Odyssey is a poem of return: the war is over now, and the struggle is for home. Going forth is necessary when we are young. We have to prove ourselves, seek our fame and fortune, find out who we are in the world so we can build what we have been given to do in our lifetime. Returning is the work of more experienced people, who, having gone forth in bright dreams, have encountered the twists and turns of pain and suffering, and so are ready to come home. Coming home sounds comforting and restful, but, as we have seen, it is not easy. In our absence powerful forces of destruction have gathered, and when we arrive we will have to do battle with them if we are to establish our rightful place. Odysseus' return, full of many twists and turns, takes twenty-four books of The Odyssey to complete! And the journey of return that we must take after we have gone forth may be just as long, just as perilous.

The Odyssey has a second, powerful hero: the sea. In world literature, the seascapes in The Odyssey are justly famous. Odysseus' adventures take him from island to island, each a small emerald shining in the vast, embracing sea. So many of the poem's most memorable lines are loving but terrifying descriptions of the sea, which is "wine dark," swells with mountainous tumult, heaves with steep valleys, blows up fearsome gales, glows in the sunrise, glistens at midday, shimmers in the moonlight. It is the province of powerful gods, who control its flow and use its power to achieve their own willful ends. Whenever the action of the story is to be advanced, the characters must quit the land and set out to sea. Doing so, they take their lives in their hands, for they never know what will happen, whether the gods will bless them and bring them safely to port, whether they will be swept away to a far land inhabited by strange and menacing creatures, or perish in the icy depths.

About the sea, the French philosopher and mystic Simone Weil says, "[it] is not less beautiful in our eyes because we know that sometimes ships are wrecked by it. On the contrary, this adds to its beauty. If it altered the movement of its waves to spare a boat, it would be a creature gifted with discernment and choice, and not this fluid, perfectly obedient to every external pressure. It is this perfect obedience that constitutes the sea's beauty."[2] The sea's perfect obedience is to the world's force, not human desire.

The sea has been Odysseus' nemesis. The sea god Poseidon has been angry with him (later we will see why), which has caused him no end of trouble. Cast off course by great storms, at the beginning of our story Odysseus is marooned on the island of Ogygia, where he is held captive by the goddess Calypso. We first meet him, listless and trapped, sitting on the beach gazing out to sea toward Ithaca, his eyes red with weeping.

There is something typically human about this sorrowful sea gazing. We all do it. We go to the beach where we gaze dreamily out to sea, searching contemplatively into its distances, watching the play of light on its ever-shifting waves. What are we looking for, or at? Gazing out to sea is pleasant, fascinating, calming. Why is looking at long, constantly moving spaces that recede out as far as the eye can see, and far beyond, so satisfying, at times compelling, yet oddly disturbing? Perhaps when we look out to sea we become Odysseus musing on our long-lost home, wondering when and how we will return.

I live near the ocean so I often look out at the sea. I never tire of it. The sea is like my life, like anyone's life: large, full of currents and depths, constantly in motion, sometimes quiet, sometimes full of whitecaps or crashing waves, and always perfectly obedient to forces I will never understand. Just as the sea is a major character in *The Odyssey,* it is a major character in our stories as well, for we also advance the action of our tale only by setting out to sea, shoving off into the unknowable, powerful, unpredictable sea of life, of time, of the world. We set out with some trepidation, because we know we can't control or even completely understand what will happen to us. We will be tossed this way and that. We will be taken somewhere whether we want to go or not, for no matter how skillfully we sail and how fervently we pray for good winds, unexpected disasters constantly occur.

Maybe we don't realize we are at the mercy of the sea. Maybe we think our own wiles and skills ensure that we will arrive safely at the port of our choosing. Of course we can, to some extent, master the sea. We can study it and come to know the patterns of its waves and currents. We can learn how to handle a boat, how to read the instruments. We can become expert sailors. But if we think that we are in charge, that we can dictate the way the rolling waves of our life stories will go, we are sadly mistaken. In fact, as any sailor knows, you cannot control the elements. If you want to sail, you must cooperate with the sea, yield to its motion, and give it all due respect. To get where you want to go, you must be attentive, fluid, and obedient, like water. Most of what makes a life satisfying and resonant lies outside the sphere of our personal skills and powers. We have been conditioned to think that we shape our lives far more than we actually do, and this is why we are so dismayed and feel so helpless when something outside our plan, outside the linear narrative flow of our life-tale, arises. To respect the sea is to trust that we can welcome life's immense and unknowable currents rather than resist them, even when they seem to be drawing us to shores we don't want to visit. We live our lives too much on small islands of conscious awareness and control. Homecoming requires that we set out to sea, as Odysseus does, and give ourselves over to its powers and its gods. The journey home cannot be predetermined. We may not always enjoy the sea's course-altering storms and paralyzing calms. But we must sail forth.

Try this exercise now if you want.

Imagine: Close your eyes and visualize the ceaselessly restless sea. There is no land in sight. Just shimmering wavelets, tipped with diamond-glinting points of light. Be with this vision, in calmness, for a few moments.

Now ask yourself, "What is the sea, the uncharted sea, of my life?" Don't press for an answer, as you might if you were being given a psychological test for a job interview. Let whatever answer just come floating to the surface of your mind, as if from the depths of the very waters your inward gaze encompasses. Maybe the answer will come in the form of a feeling, a feeling difficult to describe or understand. A feeling perhaps so subtle and vague you're not sure it's actually there. Maybe you are just making it up. Because this is an imaginative exercise, just making something up counts. Or maybe what comes is more definite than that: maybe it is a clear sense of the mystery that has always surrounded your life. Maybe you recall suddenly, after having long forgotten about it, that chance encounter, that unexpected, maybe even unwanted, series of occurrences that made all the difference in your life, that shaped it, made you what you have become. Maybe you feel a tremendous gratitude for what occurred. For without it, who knows what would have become of you? Or maybe nothing comes to mind. You just see those waves moving. And maybe you sense a storm approaching in the distance, where the sky is dark around the edges.

2 / The Paradox of Return

The journey of return is one of the great themes in the sea of human stories, found in every religious tradition. I've mentioned Judaism's notion of teshuvah, to come back, to return, to our fundamental home in God. In the Zen Oxherding pictures, the wayfarer returns to the marketplace with "gift-bestowing hands." Jesus leaves the world, and returns resurrected. In Mahayana Buddhism, to take refuge in the Buddha, the Dharma, and the Sangha, is to return to one's original nature. The word *refuge,* from the Latin, literally means "to fly back," like a bird to her nest. Odysseus' journey is also a journey of return.

Like the experience of déjà vu *(Haven't I already been here?),* journeys of return are uncanny and paradoxical. We start from home, and we return home, coming full circle. One might well wonder, What's the point of such a journey? Why leave, in the first place, if you are only going to come back to where you started from? But there is a point to this arduous and circular wandering. True, we do come back to our starting point, and we return with nothing we didn't already have before we left. Yet, at the same time there is an important difference: *we* are different, and our appreciation of what our life is and has always been is deeper.

The life of the twelfth-century Japanese Zen Master Dogen is a study in the paradox of the journey of return. Ordained while still a boy, Dogen had strong faith in the Lotus Sutra, a text in which the Buddha astonishes his followers by telling them that the spiritual journey he had previously taught them about, the heroic quest for Nirvana that leads from the world of suffering to the world of peace, through hardship and on to eventual victory, was actually a trick. In fact, since every being is by nature a Buddha, and in this sense is already at home, there is nowhere to go other than where one already is. All spiritual destinations, the Buddha tells them, are like chimerical cities, encouraging mirages produced because we are so convinced there is somewhere to go. In his past teaching, the Buddha says, he cooperated with us in our fixations about improvement and destination. Now, in the Lotus Sutra, he finally reveals the truth—the real journey is not to someplace new; it simply brings us back home to our inherent nature. Nirvana is not the end of suffering and desire that comes at the conclusion of a long process of purification and renunciation. It is simply returning to what we are.

Dogen passionately believed this teaching and yet he saw that all around him good monks and nuns were practicing mightily in quest of a Nirvana that seemed distant from them. Why? If we are already home, as the Lotus Sutra teaches, what was the point of the journey? This remained Dogen's question for many years, and it took him all the way to China and back.

The answer eluded him for so long not because it was complicated but because it was so simple it was hard to see. The purpose of spiritual practice is not to get somewhere. The purpose is to come home, to return to ourselves. And this return takes effort; necessary, joyful, continuous effort that is its own reward. We practice not to improve our situation but rather to recognize, celebrate, and express who we really are and have been all along. "Effort without desire," Dogen wrote. "Clear water all the way to the bottom; a fish swims like a fish. Vast sky transparent throughout; a bird flies like a bird."

Paradoxical though it may seem, the journey of return is one that everyone must make in his own way. Because it can be confusing, uncomfortable, and troublesome, we'd just as soon avoid it.

But we simply can't ignore, explain away, or gloss over this strange necessity to come back to ourselves. All we can do is embrace it, and manifest it in our lives through what happens to us. We must live it, though we can't direct, control, or even understand it any more than we can direct, control, or understand the rushing currents of the sea. Religious philosopher Martin Buber spoke of the essential human contradiction between what he called *It,* our dualistic, grasping physical and emotional life, and *You,* our life of love, meaning, and relationship, our spiritual side, our God side. Neither of these, he said, can be dispensed with, nor can they ever be completely teased apart. Not only do we journey, as Dogen did, as Odysseus does, back home, in the long pilgrimage of our lives; on every moment of our living we enact the journey of return as we constantly oscillate between the two sides of our human nature, *It* and *You.* This oscillation is uncomfortable for us because we can't help but prefer lives that are predictable, explainable, and secure. Where there is a paradox we want it resolved so we can put our minds at rest and move on. But there is no getting round the paradox of return.

"Man's 'religious' situation is existence in the presence," Buber writes. His use of quotation marks around the word religious here is telling. Religion, Buber is saying, is not a separate sphere of our activity, a special case of holiness, something for Sunday, and for church. Religion is our actual living, our presence, which always unfolds within the paradox of return. And this presence, he goes on, "is marked by its essential and indissoluble antinomies [that is, paradoxes]." These paradoxes are indissoluble—that is their essence. They cannot be resolved or smoothed over. There is only one way to deal with them: "Whoever would settle the conflict between these antinomies by some means short of his own life transgresses against the sense of the situation," Buber writes. Buber means that the solution to the paradox must be lived. There is no answer other than giving yourself completely to your own life. We can only live these paradoxes "ever again, ever anew, unpredictably, without any possibility of anticipation or prescription."

So we are on a journey, an immense, always new, and unpredictable journey. Our ongoing moment-to-moment life is that journey, whether we think we are going anywhere or not. This journey is necessary; it is in our very nature. It changes everything, but, paradoxically, it does this by changing nothing. The journey does not take us from somewhere to somewhere else. We go and return, yet we stay where we are. Because the journey home is an imaginative, imaginary journey, stories, myths, and metaphors help us to appreciate, activate, and uncover it. Without them we could miss the journey altogether, and that would be a shame, for this journey home contains what's most essential and most poignant in a human life. Missing the journey could also be a disaster. Remember Odysseus and the suitors: when we are absent from home, things tend to fall apart.

Sometimes along the way of our spiritual journey, we encounter sudden, shocking, and enormous changes. Sometimes equally enormous changes are so subtle and so inward that we cannot even be sure they have taken place. And sometimes for many years nothing whatsoever seems to be happening, as we simply wait—as we shall soon see the characters in *The Odyssey* wait—for our marching orders. Sometimes our journey takes us to distant countries, through many relationships, occupations, adventures. And sometimes we hardly set foot outside our house, like Emily Dickinson, who journeyed far and wide, perhaps as far as anyone ever has, without ever leaving home. The writer Eudora Welty, who lived all her life in a small town in Mississippi, wrote, "I am a writer who came of a sheltered life. A sheltered life can be a daring life as well. For all serious daring starts from within." For Julian of Norwich, the great fourteenth-century Christian mystic, the entire journey took place in a single night of manifold visions as she lay on what she thought was her deathbed. For the rest of her long life as a recluse, she continued to go over this journey again and again.

* * *

We humans are not alone in our need to make a journey of return. The sun, moon, and planets journey away and then back again, day by day and year by year. The earth journeys through the seasons and back again as it always has and always will. It is possible that the whole of the physical cosmos that sprang into being at the beginning of time is journeying forward back to that beginning, before and outside of time and being.

Other living creatures also share this journey. Sandhill cranes, for instance, like many other large and small birds, travel long and perilous distances each year, leaving home in order to return. They go by the hundreds of thousands from their winter homes in California and the American Midwest up through Canada to their summer breeding grounds in the Arctic. At summer's end they reverse course and fly back. Sandhills are the oldest birds on the planet (fossil records show individuals going back six million years) and they look it. Stately, elegant, long-billed, and long-necked, they stand about five feet tall, walk with great delicacy, and fly with a preternatural grace once they get going. I have seen hundreds of sandhills at sunset in the wintry Sacramento River delta fields of California, standing almost motionless, their quiet bodies reflected in the water that has flooded the fields after a good rain. Flock after flock comes flapping in, their thrilling ancient cry loud in the air as their long legs lower, groping for solid earth, as if they are still not used to the idea of landing after all these millennia. They take off with the same awkwardness, running along for a while on those spindly legs and finally, just barely it seems, lifting off into the air.

Another marathon migratory, the gray whale, swims over six thousand miles a year, at about five miles an hour, night and day, month after month, from feeding grounds in the Arctic back to winter breeding grounds in lagoons off the coast of Baja California in Mexico. There the whales dive and breach by the hundreds, mothers with their young swimming beside them. Large though they are, the rhythm of their rising, breathing, and plunging down is deeply peaceful and magnificent. And arctic terns, graceful white birds weighing less than two pounds, are the champion migrators of the planet. Their annual pole-to-pole homeward journey takes twenty-two thousand miles, and they spend most of their lives in the air.

In recent decades, scientists have been studying the migrations of birds and whales, and although they have learned a great deal, they cannot say precisely what cues the animals to begin their migrations. Is it a subtle change in air or water temperature, in the length of days, in the attitude of the stars in the nighttime sky? Is it the pull of the earth's gravity a little more this way than that? Maybe all these things or none of them trigger the irresistible inner impulse the animals have to do what seems impossible to us, and would no doubt seem so to them if they had the capacity to reflect on it: to fly or swim steadily for months on end. The eminent whale scientist Roger Payne did some detailed studies years ago that seemed to raise doubts about the gray whales' need to migrate to complete their life cycle. He found that every year some whales did not migrate south and instead managed to bear their young in the Arctic, in the lee of glaciers. Why go all that way just to turn around and come back?

One of the underlying reasons that birds and whales migrate is that the earth is off-kilter. The axis on which the earth spins in its daily rotation is not oriented at right angles to the sun, but tilted at a messy 23 degrees 27 minutes. This is why the seasons change: in winter the earth tilts 23 degrees, 27 minutes away from the sun; in summer 23 degrees 27 minutes toward it. The effect of this tilt is least pronounced at the equator, most pronounced at the poles, which is why the Arctic has such long days in summer and short days in winter. Long days mean more light, which means more and larger plants, which means more insects, more food for birds who need maximum fuel for the breeding season. Food for gray whales depends on the upwelling of organic matter from the ocean waters below, which depends on the power of the ocean currents, which are stronger toward the poles. But the short northern winter days offer little food and bitter cold, which is difficult for raising young. So because the earth is off-kilter, birds fly north and then south and whales swim north and then south. It's as if the planet were a bowl of loose marbles tipped this way then that way, the marbles sliding back and forth.

The earth is naturally off-kilter. That is how it works, that is its nature. The human heart is also off-kilter, and this is its nature, too, this is how it works. Like birds and whales, like the stars, planets, and all the physical world, we too have the unstoppable impulse to make the journey of return. Birds and whales simply go when it is time. They have no trouble getting started, no discomfort, no resistance. We, on the other hand, who can think and speak and so imagine other possibilities, are more likely to complain, to be disappointed, frustrated, uncomfortable, and confused with the effort of our return. But we are not really so different from the stars and other animals. We also must fulfill our nature. Though it may be hard for us to admit it, we have no other choice. The earth, in fact, spins exactly as it ought to. It is "off-kilter" only from our point of view. And we suffer and struggle exactly as we need to in our paradoxical, poignant, and lovely journey home.

3 / Waiting

Odysseus' journey home does not begin with Odysseus. After the opening lines sketch out Odysseus' character, the poem shifts its scene, for the next four books, to Ithaca, where his son Telemachus is stuck. Restless to begin his own journey outward, Telemachus must remain at home, with nothing to do, stalled and frustrated. He must stand impotently by while the suitors feast on Odysseus' cattle, goats, and stocks of wine, and his mother weaves by day and secretly unweaves by night her father-in-law Laertes' shroud. So everyone is waiting: Penelope, the suitors, and Laertes, who has not been able to die.

Like the others, Telemachus is stalled because of Odysseus' absence. The other veterans returned from Troy long ago; their houses are in order, their sons have gone on with their lives. Only Odysseus remains missing, his whereabouts unknown. Nor is it clear whether he is alive or dead, so Telemachus cannot even mourn. Rumors abound, which only make matters worse. Day by day Telemachus can do nothing but wait, with no end in sight, while time—and the literal substance of the household—is running out. So *The Odyssey,* the greatest of all literary journeys of return, begins not with a crisis, a leave-taking, a challenge, or an adventure, but with absence, waiting, uncertainty, frustration.

Maybe this sounds familiar to you. It does to me. It accurately suggests that the journey home doesn't begin with the clarity that crisis and danger can bring. Even when the beginning seems clearly initiated by a crisis, in retrospect one realizes that, before the crisis, there was a long, vague, dark preparatory period characterized by a barely perceptible feeling of absence or lack, an uneasy sense that one was waiting to begin one's real life. And even when the crisis comes, it quickly seems as if it is not the crisis that is really at issue, it's all that the crisis has dredged up and revealed—the much larger, unexamined, and possibly unanswerable questions to which it gives rise—that in the end matter most.

We all know a crisis when we see it, a death, an illness, loss of a job or career, breakup of a family or relationship, and we are all spurred into action by such crises—if we are not entirely defeated by them. But after the dust of frenzied activity settles, and we are finally able to feel our way into what we have been through, we realize just how unhinged we have become. We can't go back to business as usual, for we sense that we no longer fit into our former life. We need a new life. But we don't know how to find it. There's nothing else to do right now but stay where we are and wait, frustrating though this may be.

Without a crisis to launch you on your journey, life simply proceeds as usual. This may be worse than suffering a crisis. Day succeeds day, week succeeds week, possibly years or decades go by and there is the dawning of a feeling inside us—sometimes it dawns only in our dreams, or in small barely noticeable moments at the margins of our lives—that something is not right. We are vaguely aware that we are living in a holding pattern, that we have yet to commit ourselves to our real lives. Maybe long ago we thought we had seized the day, thought we had gone forward bravely with decisions and plans, but now we see that we had been leading with our heads rather than our hearts and our guts, and our heads were too much influenced by our fears and by our conditioning. We chose lives we thought we liked or wanted, or were at least socially acceptable, but never thought to discover what we were absolutely driven to: in other words, though we may look fine outwardly, inwardly we feel as if we haven't actually begun to live. And we're not even sure of *this!* Even when we think this feeling of being stalled is true, we have no clue what to do about it. Most of the time, of course, we're not thinking about it. We're just going on with our to-do lists, with all the various requirements, plans, and tasks of our lives in the world. But every now and then, when we are alone and quiet, the restlessness comes on us. We feel like foreigners in our own lives, like refugees from some other life in some other world, but no, this couldn't be so, could it? It's an uncomfortable feeling. We don't like it. So we try to avoid being alone and quiet; we occupy ourselves with noise and gossip and, especially, stories, lots of stories, keeping ourselves plenty busy with weaving (and unweaving at night what we have woven during the day), eating cattle, and drinking wine, so we won't have to face the emptiness and uncertainty that's just beneath the surface. Day by day we deplete our substance; time is running out, we know that it is, we're stuck, stalled, and the situation is very unclear and definitely beyond our control.

For most of my years at the Zen Center I had the job of guiding the many people who came there as full-time residential students. I found that often people came, not out of a burning interest in Zen Buddhism, but simply because they didn't know what else to do. Many of them were lost in some way, stalled and stuck. Some were young, just beginning their grown-up lives, and some were older, and their lives had fallen apart or they had broken apart their lives, because they knew something wasn't right. The friends and relatives of these people may have worried about their going to the Zen Center, where they would be learning no useful marketable skills or furthering their life aims in any concrete way. The Zen Center didn't even offer the benefits of a therapeutic or human potential community, where at least, presumably, you were going to be healed or learn something about yourself. At the Zen Center you would merely practice meditation and chanting, attend lectures on Zen, and do plenty of work. From any objective or even subjective point of view, all this, while possibly interesting, is more or less a waste of time.

But I felt quite differently. It didn't bother me that people stumbled into the Zen Center in their confusion, sometimes not even realizing how lost they were, and probably looking for something they were not going to find. I believe that, below their surface confusion, a deeper wisdom had guided them there. Although the Zen Center would teach them little, and do almost nothing for their résumés, their coming there was precisely the right thing for them to do. Unable to go along with life choices that looked outwardly to be moving them forward, these people were coming to the Zen Center, whether they realized it or not, simply to wait. They were coming to do nothing, to go nowhere, but simply to wait. Sometimes the waiting was frustrating to them; they often wondered what they were doing there, and they often complained, wanting the Zen Center to give them more than it ever could. Nevertheless, it was a great advantage to them to be where they were: dissatisfied, frustrated, and stuck as they often felt, at least they had no illusions that something was going on. They couldn't fool themselves about their lives, or distract themselves somehow. At the Zen Center they had to face themselves, right where they were, each and every day. There was nothing else going on.

This being stuck and stalled, this waiting and going nowhere, may sound terrible, but it's not. The journey of return begins with stasis, with uncertainty. Do not rush to clear this up, much as you, like Telemachus, may want to. At this point, here and now, admit your situation, know it for what it is, and be willing to endure it. Waiting may be uncomfortable, but it is profound and necessary. Most of us are too impatient to wait. We can't sit still for it and rush forward with more plans and schemes, action of all sorts. But where does this all actually get us, but into lives that are elaborate avoidance mechanisms?

Sometimes, we are willing to wait, but don't know how. We have no tools or techniques. So we strategize, thinking through our next moves. We call that waiting, but it isn't real waiting. Real waiting requires that we drop all goals and plans and be willing simply to sit at the edge of our seats, as Zen monastics do, alert and aware, pregnant with anticipation, but not anticipation *for* something. Waiting is another paradox: we are waiting but not for something. We are waiting for nothing.

Most of us find this intolerable. Impossible. We don't want to be passive, we want to be active, even proactive. My father used to have a tie clasp with the letters YCDBSOYA engraved on it. It was meant to pique your curiosity. The letters stood for "You can't do business sitting on your ass." How true! We won't get anywhere sitting on our rear ends; we have to get up and shake the world a little bit if we are to go forward with our lives. We are not fools. We are willing to wait sometimes because we understand that good things don't always come all of a sudden or exactly when we want them, that patience is sometimes required. But to make a virtue of waiting—to do nothing but wait—for how long we don't know—and to wait precisely for nothing! This makes no sense. It's a waste of time. It's uncomfortable simply to *be* there with nothing to look forward to and nothing to do. So, instead, we distract ourselves with a million meaningless details and activities that make us feel as if we are doing something worthwhile.

Simone Weil is the great prophet of waiting. "There is a special way of waiting upon truth, setting our hearts upon it, yet not allowing ourselves to go out in search of it," she writes. "There is a way of waiting, when we are writing, for the right word to come of itself at the end of our pen, while we merely reject all inadequate words."[1] Weil called this waiting for nothing at all "waiting for God." I am sure she was thinking of the prophet Isaiah, who wrote, "They who wait for God will find renewed strength, as eagles grow new plumes; they shall run and not grow weary, march and not grow faint."[2]

So *The Odyssey* doesn't begin with a bang, a flurry of heroic activity. It begins with Telemachus' waiting. Your odyssey begins the same way. When you are finally ready to stop for a while, as people who came to the Zen Center were willing to do, you will enter the profound uncertainty of your own waiting. And that waiting will go on for some time without any assurances of when—or if—it will end.

Imagine you are Telemachus. That is, imagine that your life, whatever it is or seems to be, is not what it must be or will be. Imagine that a new life is there within you, already taking shape within the structure of the life you think you are living, but you don't know what the new life is and there's no way you can find out what it is. There's nothing to do but simply wait. Wait and allow this new life to ripen within you.

Imagine the new life as a spot or point of light deep in your belly. If it is dim at first, make it brighter with your breathing. Breathe it, imagine it, to brightness. Breathe in its energy when you inhale; breathe out its power when you exhale. Maybe you can't exactly see it, but you can feel it in your breathing.

Keep breathing for a while in this way. Don't sit comfortably or in a relaxed manner. Sit literally on the edge of your seat, with your spine lengthened, your head erect, eyes closed but pointed straight ahead. Do you feel anxious or overly curious? Breathe through that feeling. Don't try to make it go away. Just let yourself wait, with the feeling of the new life warm within your belly. Sit this way for as long as you like. See if, as the time passes, anything within you changes. If you suddenly have a sense of what the new life is, some image of it, or even some particular call to action, notice that but let it go. That's not it. It's just a passing image, a stray thought or impulse. Keep on waiting, waiting for nothing. Don't expect anything to happen. Be willing to wait like this forever. Be willing to wait each moment as if it were already forever.

If, after sitting this way for a while, you are moved to go to your journal to write, do so. But don't think about what you are going to write. Do not make thoughts your aim. Follow Simone Weil's instruction to let the right word "come of itself at the edge of your pen." Reject all the wrong words, all the conditioned, expected, desired, acceptable, words. Let yourself wait for a word that wants to be there, whether you want it or not. If no word comes, that's fine. But if a word, or a phrase, or a sentence, comes, write it. And wait for further instructions. One word, one phrase, one sentence, may be enough.

———

Each day is all.

4 / Speak Your Grief

Telemachus' waiting finally comes to an end when he feels moved to call a community assembly. Regular meetings had been a feature of life on Ithaca when Odysseus was there, but none has been held since his departure. Surprised by the unexpected summons, the Achaeans of Ithaca come quickly. Telemachus enters, takes his father's seat, and remains silent as one of the older men opens the conversation by wondering who called the assembly and why. Bursting with what he has to say, Telemachus leaps to his feet to address the group:

> I was the one who called us all together.
> Something wounds me deeply . . .
> not news I've heard of an army on the march,
> word I've caught firsthand so I can warn you now,
> or some other public matter I'll disclose and argue.
> No, the crisis is my own. Trouble has struck my house—
> a double blow. First, I have lost my noble father
> who ruled among you years ago, each of you here,
> and kindly as a father to his children.
>   But now this,
> a worse disaster that soon will grind my house down . . . [1]

Telemachus goes on to indict the suitors for their irresponsible, destructive behavior, against which he has no defense. At the end of his impassioned speech he is so upset he throws down the speaker's scepter and bursts into tears. The assembly of Odysseus' peers and countrymen is full of pity, and all remain silent for a while, ashamed, for during all the years the suitors have been overrunning Odysseus' household, no one has ever said a word about it. Until now, no one acknowledged or named the injustice. Afraid of what the suitors—scions of powerful families—might do in retaliation, the Achaeans looked the other way, colluding, as it were, with this slow destruction of the natural order of things, unwilling to challenge the suitors or even to take note of what has been happening. In this conspiracy of silence, Telemachus has been stewing, his life on hold. But now, finally, since no one else will do it—since no one else *can* do it—Telemachus speaks his private grief publicly.

Aside from evoking their pity, however, Telemachus' words seem to have little effect on his timid countrymen. Representatives of the suitors speak up, defending their right to do what they are doing and blaming Penelope for her stalling deception (her weaving and unweaving), which they have found out. But suddenly, in the midst of the debate, there is a dramatic portent: two eagles appear in the sky, swoop, and attack each other, an astonishing display of power and violence. Clearly, Telemachus' speaking, however ineffective it may have been in political terms, is making a difference on a higher level—in the heavens, where the gods live.

Telemachus' long-deferred outburst might well mirror the overdue expression any one of us might make, as we open our throats to let the world know that we are stuck, that we are suffering, that we have been bearing—possibly without fully knowing it ourselves—a great grief for a long time. Like the good, polite, and timid Achaeans of Ithaca, our friends have been colluding with the suitors, never asking us the questions that might evoke our real feelings, not wanting to get close to that tender spot in us, because it seems so challenging, so frightening, and because it might draw forth similar pain in them. It is possible that, for our whole lives, we have had no one to talk to, no one who could listen in a way that would allow the feelings and words we needed to express, but couldn't find a way to say—at least not until now, not until our waiting has ripened it for us. Even if someone had pointed out our condition to us, it wouldn't have helped. We wouldn't have been ready to hear, for we had not yet come to grips with our soul. This is work only we can do; no one can do it for us. But now, on our own, after long waiting, we stand up in the assembly and express ourselves. Trouble has struck our houses a double blow: first, we feel the absence of a true path for our souls. Second, we are grieving over the gnawing ongoing dissolution of our birthright as, day by day, we fail to seize the moment of our lives. At this point we have no solution. Like Telemachus we have miles to go, encounters to seek, before we can even begin to address what is eating us up alive. But for now, simply to express ourselves, to speak, shout, sob, moan, cry out our truth—from the heart, from the gut, from the throat—is enough. Although no one rushes forward to help us, and nothing seems to have changed, eagles clash above us in the sky, signs and portents of what's to come.

No matter our circumstances, life is inevitably a series of sudden or gradual losses punctuated by periods of respite that are actually just staging areas for the losses still to come. But never mind the obvious losses that any life brings. Even when things are thrilling, joyful, merry, and bright, there is still loss. For what is a moment of time if not a moment of time that is passing, and what is the getting or accomplishing or experiencing of anything, if not the occasion for the slow disengagement with the delight one feels, a disengagement and disenchantment that begins at the very moment the delight appears. Real life does not match the naïve descriptions of it we have received in the press notices passed on to us by parents, teachers, and social institutions. Real life is contradictory and problematic. If you are willing to look unflinchingly, you will see that even happiness depends on loss. The gratitude, love, or joy that we feel depends on the temporariness of things. The rarity of that for which we are grateful is why it delights us so.

Still, we grab for delight and love and joy when we can get

it, and we try, like the Achaeans of the Ithacan assembly, to look the other way when grief is afoot. This is normal behavior in normal human civilization. In fact, one could define civilization as an elaborate, engaging mechanism for avoiding basic truths about our lives. It's normal for us to harbor such tremendous caches of grief and sorrow inside ourselves, which we have been saving over a lifetime. Like Telemachus, we have to wait for the feelings to gather and ripen within us until the time comes for them to rise to the surface—until finally we are ready to burst open with them. We call an assembly and speak our hearts.

What I have been saying is more or less what the Buddha indicated when he set forth his first Noble Truth: that all conditioned existence is suffering. Life is suffering not because life is always so terrible, but because life is so radically temporary—every single moment of it. This is life's nature: there's nothing that appears that we won't lose, including all our thoughts, all our friends and loved ones, our body and our feelings. It's the first truth because going onward in our journey home requires that we start out realistically, with an honest appraisal of the situation as it is. As long as we deny, obscure, avoid, or cover up with distractions, abstractions, and fear, there's no way we can even begin. But if we wait long enough to really see it, and express what we feel about it, naming it and making it our own emotionally as well as intellectually, then we can move forward into the second, third and fourth Noble Truths: We can see, understand, and express the cause of suffering; we can effect the end of suffering; and there's a way to go about accomplishing this.

Expressing ourselves is a tricky business and involves more than it may seem at first blush. It's not simply a matter of opening your mouth and letting your "winged words" fly out, as *The Odyssey* puts it. We talk all the time, thousands of words a day, but how much of our talk is real expression? To express ourselves truly we need first to feel ourselves deeply, which is what we have been waiting for. Then we need the inner occasion that will draw forth what needs to be said, that will shape it into something more than a bright idea, a hope, a wish, or a mere personal insight. And we need witnesses, those who will really listen, with full sympathy and without fear, and give us permission and encouragement to speak. Finally, we need the outer occasion, the right moment and circumstances in which what we need to say can be said, for what needs to be said can only be said at the right time, and in the right place.

Some years ago, all these elements came together in my life, enabling me to express my grief in a way that made a big difference. It was on the day of the bar mitzvah of our twin sons, Aron and Noah, an event that my father had been, literally, living for for some months. Quite ill, my father was very close to death and struggling to remain alive—not because he wanted to live, for his life was pretty miserable, and he did want to die—but so that he could come to this bar mitzvah, the first of his grandchildren's bar mitzvahs and certainly the only one he had any chance of attending. A loyal, observant Jew with a strong sense of family continuity, my father was determined to be present for this occasion no matter what. So, weighing about ninety pounds, barely able to stand, he had flown across the country for the ceremony, during most of which he'd needed to lie down. When it came time for him to present our sons with the traditional prayer shawls, he had to be held up by people on either side of him, and though his voice was weak, he spoke with a great deal of joy and conviction.

After the ceremony, my father was too exhausted to go to the party and needed to rest. I took him in the car to a quiet place nearby, overlooking the ocean. By this time in our lives, he and I were getting along fine, but it had not always been so. Like many fathers and sons, we had had our differences. His need for me to be a man made in his image and my need to be an independent person—combined with many unconscious aggressive male passions that I am sure were swirling around in both of us—made for a rocky ten or twenty years during my adolescence and young manhood. But on this day I really appreciated him and I think he appreciated me, and, because of the special quality of the occasion, and of the inner work that both of us had done over the years, each in our own ways, we were able to express to each other how sorry we were for the past, which we would never be able to change, and how much we loved each other now. Time for us was clearly short. So we spoke urgently of our grief and our love. And the words, few and halting though they may have been, gave us at last a sense of repair and fullness, as if the relationship we had both been born to build had been completed. That would be our last conversation. Within two months my father was dead.

These days, as I continue to teach Zen outside the traditional context of monastic life, I am trying to see what will work to bring ordinary people in the ordinary world to the sort of deeper, fuller living that Zen promises. I have found that it is of crucial importance to create opportunities for people to express themselves fully. In traditional Zen practice the teacher gives a talk and the students listen. Sometimes, after the talk, the students have a chance to ask questions, but usually not. In recent years it's become clear to me that students need to do more than absorb teachings and ask clarifying questions. They need to stand up in the assembly and speak their hearts. So at my weekly dharma seminar we have a meditation period and a Zen talk, but after the talk, instead of answering questions, I ask them. The students gather into groups to explore for themselves the questions I have posed (or other perhaps more important questions of their own). They speak and listen carefully to each other. I have often been astonished at what has been expressed at these occasions, at the subtlety and depth of people's concerns. Witnessing these conversations has convinced me that we all have much within us to express, but that we don't know this because the invitation to express it is so seldom given. Expression is healing. It opens us, propelling us forth into our lives. It's not so much a matter of ideas or even of feelings, for expression is more than a cognitive or an emotional act. Yet somehow the simple act of speaking truly, out loud and to others, inspires us, enabling us finally to point our prow out to sea as we set forth onward for the journey.

Imagine you are in the presence of someone whom you respect and love, who feels the same way about you. A person who is interested in what you think and feel, but doesn't assume (as so many do) that he or she knows in advance what that is, but instead is humble, curious, and fully receptive. (If there is no such person in your life—and don't be dismayed; this is not so unusual—conjure one up.) Feel the person's presence, feel her gaze, listen to her voice as she says to you, "How is it with you these days? What is uppermost in your heart?"

Drink in these questions deeply, let them settle within you. And then, without rehearsing, without referencing all the voices of approval and disapproval so long lodged within you, let yourself speak. Speak out loud. Let the words come, almost as if you were not directing them, as if they were coming from a place in you you've never experienced before. If it helps you to get started you can begin with the phrase "This is what I really want to say . . ." Once you begin, keep talking. If you run out of things to say repeat the last words spoken over and over again until more words come. Speak until there is nothing left to say. You will know when that is.

Another way to do this is to write a letter to the person you love. Make up your mind in advance that you will not be sending the letter so you need not be constrained by what you think the person—real or imagined—might want to hear. As in the last exercise inspired by Simone Weil, practice waiting for the right word, but, this time, once the right word comes, keep on writing, repeating words, even nonsense words, if you get stuck, until you are unstuck. Feel what it's like to express your heart, after long suffering silence, to the great assembly.

5 / False Stories

What precipitated the abrupt end of Telemachus' waiting? To answer this we have to take a step backward in our story.

The ancient Greek gods frequently met in heavenly council to review the troubles and stupidities of mortals. At an assembly that takes place in Book 1 of *The Odyssey*, Zeus complains bitterly, What nerve mortals have! Despite all the portents and fair warnings we gods provide, they persist in giving in to their greed and violence, and when they are punished for their crimes, just as we warned them they would be, they have the gall to blame us, as if it were our fault! Outrageous!

Attending this assembly is the goddess Athena, Odysseus' great protector. She agrees that passion-bound mortals who foolishly cross the gods' desires ought to be punished. But why should noble Odysseus be cursed by fate for so long through no fault of his own? she protests. "Have you no care for *him* in your lofty heart? Did he never win your favor with sacrifices / burned beside the ships on the broad plain of Troy? / Why, Zeus, why so dead set against Odysseus?"[1] Zeus agrees to free Odysseus from captivity and let him go home where his presence is so sorely needed. He sends the messenger god Hermes to Ogygia (where Odysseus is still gazing sadly at the sea) to tell Calypso to let Odysseus go. For her part, Athena straps on her golden sandals and "wings over the waves and boundless earth with a rush of gusting winds" to Ithaca, where her task is to spur the despondent Telemachus on to action. Disguised as a mortal (as the gods usually are when they appear in the human world), a sailor, Athena strides into the chaotic banquet hall where the suitors are feasting, partying, and now also gambling. She hangs up her heavy spear. Telemachus greets her, offers her food and drink, as is customary, and then, taking her aside to a quiet corner, asks politely where she's from and what brings her to Ithaca. Athena now tells the first of many false stories that abound in *The Odyssey*.

The story is full of plausible details: Her name is Mentes, a seafaring merchant, on a mission to trade iron for bronze. Mentes claims to know Odysseus from long ago, to have family connections with him, and encourages Telemachus not to lose heart, that surely Odysseus is alive, will return, and that he, Telemachus, must stand up for himself and act like the man he now is. Call an assembly, she tells him; speak your frustration and your grief with your full voice; let the suitors know you're not going to take this anymore, and then find a ship (I will help you!), and go forth to seek news of your father. If you hear he is alive, then come back and brave out one more year. If you hear he is dead, then return and mourn him as any son should, and give your mother over to some worthy groom. "Then, once you've sealed those matters, seen them through, / think hard, reach down deep into your heart and soul / for a way to kill these suitors in your house, / by stealth or in open combat," she tells him. "You must not cling to your boyhood any longer— / it's time you were a man."[2] Stirred by this inspiring, energizing encounter, Telemachus calls the assembly the very next day.

This telling of false tales is a major feature of *The Odyssey*. Eloquent, devious, convincing, and quick, Odysseus himself is a master of the false story. Even Telemachus, an innocent young man, often withholds or obscures his identity when he meets people. He will do this when he journeys out to seek word of his father from Nestor, Odysseus' old comrade in arms at Troy. Even when Odysseus and Penelope are finally united toward the end of *The Odyssey*, Odysseus, in disguise as a beggar, does not reveal his identity. When he finally does, Penelope doubts it. False stories, withheld stories, doubtful stories, even true stories that are doubted, are a crucial characteristic of *The Odyssey*.

Most of our various life stories are also false stories, doubtful stories, partial stories. We usually do not intend to be deceptive, but it is often necessary. In order to go on with our lives, to get from one place to another, we have to hold up a story at some point: this is who I am, this is what I want, this is where I am going. To grow up, enter society, interact with others, sail forth into our lives, we need stories, identities, plausible characters, and forward-moving narratives that advance a plot. But even the stories we tell ourselves to propel our lives forward are, inevitably, altogether or partly false. Sometimes we say who we are to convince ourselves or someone else, but it's not really who we are. Sometimes we come close to saying who we really are but no one believes us. Sometimes we don't say who we are because it is not the time or place for it. As we practice with our own story, we recognize that we have many stories, true ones, doubtful ones, false ones—as does everyone we meet.

Is there a true story? Or, at least, a story that is true for now? And, true or not, what does it mean to us to live our stories? Seeking the answers to these questions is what impels us forward on the journey of return: we need to tell the truest story we can find for the life we are living now.

But no story can be completely true. As long as we are alive our story is always doubtful because it is not over yet. What happens next might change the entire story, just as, sometimes, at the end of a novel, something happens that changes your whole notion of what the novel has been about. When our life ends the true story may be known, but not fully even then—because others will tell our story as they need to tell it, and they will retell it according to their shifting needs, making it true and false and doubtful all over again. Think of the world's great stories: the story of Buddha or Jesus or Odysseus. These are true or false or doubtful stories, told over and over again in different ways according to our human needs, to help us to find some wisdom, some order, and some peace.

It's interesting that it takes deception to get things going for Telemachus. One does not expect this. Almost all discussions of the spiritual journey are couched in terms of goodness, virtue, and truth. They speak of straightforwardness, honesty, authenticity, and love. But we human beings are not so straightforward. Rather, exactly like Odysseus, we are a bit crooked, full of twists and turns. When we deny our crookedness, pretending to be more upright than we actually are, the consequences are usually not good. More often than not, the people who evidence the most virtue, the most goodness, the most kindness and piety are, in the end, the most screwed up, and cause the most harm in spiritual communities and elsewhere. This is not only because virtue's power has its shadow side, which can emerge unexpectedly to trip you up when you are looking the other way. No, there is more to it than that. It is also because, no matter how innocent or smart you are, and no matter how hard you try, all your words and deeds are partial, to some extent hidden, and therefore essentially untrue. What we identify as virtuous or true really isn't that, it's just an idealized picture we have concocted, a false tale, another version, maybe a prettier, cleaned-up version, of our human confusion. Even the many heroes we had in the second half of the twentieth century, people like John F. Kennedy, Martin Luther King Jr., or Pope John Paul II, who were in some sense truly heroes worthy of our veneration, lived lives that included other realities: Kennedy had his many extramarital affairs; King was desperately unable to end his sexual wanderings even as the FBI stalked him; the compassionate pope mercilessly crushed his opponents in the Church. In fact all our stories of virtue and goodness—all our stories, period—are always partial and provisional. There's always another side, another angle, something left untold, undiscovered, perhaps untellable and undiscoverable.

In itself, the partiality or ambiguity of our stories is not necessarily a problem. The problem is that we think our stories are one-dimensionally true, and we expect them to be true in that way. We think we're virtuous or honest; we expect this of ourselves, build an identity on it, and when we find out it's not actually so we become disappointed, and resolve to be more honest, more good, more true, thereby starting the whole cycle of self-deception and disappointment all over again. We will never find a true story. We will only find, perhaps, a more plausible false story that will disappoint us sooner or later if we believe it too earnestly.

In the inner life, which is to say in life in general (for where is there ever an outer life that isn't also an inner life?), everything is more or less true and everything is more or less false. People are forever looking for who they really are, or what they really want. But what does "really" mean? In fact, it is better not to seek "reallys" and instead to accept that our stories are provisional and partial, and to make use of these stories, limited as they are, to spur us forward into lives that matter—lives that maybe we don't understand and can't control but that we really live, or rather, that live us. The story of my life, like the story of your life, is a false story. Trying to make that story true will only frustrate me. I am better off simply recognizing it as a false story, and using that story, as far as it goes, to pull me forward into whatever comes next.

In the end perhaps the true story, the story that awaits us when we return home, transcends the necessary false stories, while including them all. At that point we will not need to cling to this or that story as true—or as false. Instead we will be patient with whatever story is useful for the moment, confident in the fundamental reality behind it. Zen master Hakuun was once famously (if falsely) accused of fathering a child with a village girl. Her parents banged angrily on the temple door, thrust the infant inside, and chewed out the old, supposedly celibate monk for his sexual outrage. "Oh, is that so?" Hakuun is said to have responded. When, months later the girl admitted her lie and the chagrined parents returned, bowing and apologizing, to take back the child,

Hakuun again said, "Oh, is that so?" just as impressed and amused with the story of the saintly priest as he was with the story of the dirty old cleric.

We use false stories in many ways. We use them to get necessary things done, as Athena does when she appears as Mentes in order to convince Telemachus, and later when she appears as an impressive Achaean prince for the purpose of garnering a crew for Telemachus' ship. The false tales of our heroes encourage us toward our own achievements by giving us some faith in human possibility. However false our own stories may be, when we share them we find the companionship and encouragement we need for our journey. False stories are our main means of communication, of sharing our lives, even if we are never quite sharing them truthfully, or fully, enough. If we waited for the real truth and the real intimacy, we'd be waiting a long time. There are people who insist on true stories, and wait possibly a lifetime for them, a lifetime in which nothing at all happens. I am reminded of psychologist D. W. Winnicott's concept of the "good-enough mother" who expresses enough love to nurture a child without damaging him or her, even though she may mix her expressions of love with a certain amount of neurosis. Similarly, our false stories (for instance, that we love when we partly love and partly do not love; that we have courage when we are mostly afraid) are true enough. They give us the push we need to go forward into our lives with others.

Go back again to the meditation we practiced on page 16. Contemplate it again, as you now think of the many stories, true or false, or simultaneously true and false, that make up the impossible-to-encompass story of your life. Take a moment to savor these stories. You as hero, you as lover, you as victim. Possibly even you as archvillain; you as guilty, fearful, unworthy. You as infant, you as child, you as young man or woman; you as older man or woman. As husband, wife, mother, father, son, daughter. As outer or inner warrior. So many stories, all true, all false, all you and all not you, all necessary. Each has had its function. Each has conveyed its little piece of truth, held up its little kernel of deception. And behind the stories, what do you find? Take a moment to consider this. Close your eyes. Breathe into the silence. Take your time for this. Be curious but don't look too hard.

What do you find? What is the true self behind all the stories? Can you find anything there at all? Possibly yes and possibly no. The sense of this true self behind and within you seems inescapable. You can feel it. Beneath the stories this True Person lurks. This True Person is you—of whom all stories are told.

6 / Leaving Home

Wwe long to come home because we don't feel at home where we are, and we have a memory of home that beckons us with its rightness. Like Odysseus, we know that, whatever it takes, we have to go back, because our lives and the lives of those we love depend on it.

Why did we leave home in the first place? We left home because we had to, however conscious or unconscious of that need we were at the time. We needed to leave so that we could become the person we were meant to be. We knew we couldn't remain in our family, in our hometown, in our simple and naïve heart, forever. When we were in the womb something made us uncomfortable and pushed us out into the harsh world. We went on with our life until something made us uncomfortable at home, and forced us outward and onward. There is no *Odyssey* without an *Iliad* ("a poem of force," Simone Weil called the *Iliad*), and there is no returning without leaving.

Almost all great religious traditions work with the theme of "leaving home." To join the Buddhist order is to become a "home leaver," renouncing your worldly home and family for a life without possessions, home, or fixed identity—a life of wandering. In this, Buddhist monastics imitate the Buddha, who, disturbed by the inescapable indignities of sickness, old age, and death that he sees all around him, leaves home in the middle of the night, seeking a way out of the impossible predicament we call living. In the Bible, Abraham is rousted out of his home by God, who commands him to "leave your father's house and all that you know and hold dear and go to the land that I will show you." Jesus leaves the loving support of his disciples to enter the desert for forty days and forty nights (imitating his people, who abruptly left their sorry homes in Egypt for the desert where they wandered forty years, and Moses, who prepared to lead them with his own long wilderness exile). Mohammed flees Medina. Native Americans go off alone into the mountains to fast and seek visions. So, too, Telemachus finally leaves home secretly, sailing away under cover of darkness: "And the prow sheared through the night and into dawn."[1]

Leaving home means setting aside all we know, all that is secure, authoritative, comfortable, and binding, and shoving off for parts unknown with no road map and no guarantee of finding your way. Though it can look like—and even in some cases can be—a form of running away, an act of cowardice, real home-leaving is courageous, requiring heart and force. To go forward you must leave everything behind, and even though the past may seem to be persistent, lodged as it is in our very bones, it is one thing to be bound up by the past, doomed to repeat it or to be held back by it endlessly, and another to use it as a springboard for a journey that goes beyond—to where, one can never know.

So, leaving home, often literally and always metaphorically, is a necessary step along the path of the journey of return. After your long waiting, which is an inner ripening, comes expression, a wail or a scream or a poem, and then action; you climb into your boat, crew and provisions in place, and push off into the dark sea for parts unknown. What does it take to motivate you to leave behind everything, and to set forth on a dangerous mission without knowing where you are going or precisely why? Is fear enough, fear that life is growing shorter by the day and that you haven't really begun to live? Fear that the foundations of the life you have built are so shaky that you need another approach, a new foundation? Or fear simply that you have not loved and that after all these years you have no idea who you really are? Fear is a good motivator. Probably a certain amount of it is necessary. But fear alone is not enough. Home-leaving requires a vision more stimulating and more sustaining than the vague notion that we have to "get a life."

After rousing Telemachus out of his doldrums, motivating him to go forth into his real life, Athena leaves, literally flying away like a bird:

> *But as she went she put a new spirit in him*
> *A new dream of his father, clearer now,*
> *So that he marveled to himself* [2]

In leaving home we must do more than simply flee; we also must move toward something uplifting and challenging, however vague it may be. And even if, like Telemachus, we receive this vision through contact with others, the vision can't be someone else's property; we have to make it our own. And it must be powerful enough to motivate us, to awaken us from our slumber, to turn our paralyzing fear into action. Though our adventures on the open sea might not be identifiable to the outward eye, and though our setting forth will result in the end in our coming back to where we started from, we don't know this at first, and the journey is real to us, desperate, crucial, and difficult. So we need a considerable force to get us started.

Telemachus finds this force in a "new dream of his father," that is, a new confidence that his father is alive, that knowledge of him is possible, and that he must seek it. As a son, a father, and a spiritual teacher who is often mistaken for a father, I know how powerfully motivating (for good and for ill) a vision of "the father" can be, however ambiguous its unconscious effects. In our time we have necessarily criticized what we call patriarchy, the social order that customarily places men in positions of unassailable power, with all the social and psychic injustice this inevitably brings. Traditional patriarchy also has underlain our spiritual realities as well. God has been seen as "the father," seat of spiritual power and leading force of our inner journeying. Men have been considered to be in charge of religious life, women relegated to secondary roles. We want now to overcome this ancient bias, to elevate mothers as well as fathers, and to go further than this, beyond hierarchy and control, toward a sense of personal empowerment inside and out.

Despite this important and ubiquitous contemporary imperative, we can't deny the persistent power in our psyches of the archetypal figure of the father (beyond any particular father or male person). The relationship with the father figure, as I suggested earlier when I spoke of my own father, is fraught with undercurrents of passion and violence. Yet we can't dispense with it, any more than we can dispense with our biological father, no matter how disastrous a force he has been in our lives. The father, as well as the mother, gives us life, a genetic code and a psychological imprint with which we spend our lives working. Along with the mother, he is "author" of our lives and, if we want to claim that authorship in his stead, we can only do it through negotiation, by transferring his power to ourselves. Although we may prefer to forget about the father, to skip this thorny negotiation, one way or another we must go through this step, however painful and scary it might be, if we want to find our own authority.

The father is also something larger than a powerful male archetype in our lives; he is a metaphor that contains our feeling for the world we enter when we leave home. Formidable and foreboding, that world bears down on us with its full intimidating weight. That weight had been dragging down Telemachus, but when he shoves off in his boat to seek news of his father, he is inspired with new possibilities. No longer stuck with the absent father as the stum-

bling block, the heavy inert dragging force preventing all movement and reducing him to impotent complainant, Telemachus can
now see in the absence and unknown fate of his father a creative
dream calling him onward. We can put this in the context of the
four Buddhist truths: in finally leaving home, Telemachus digests
the first Noble Truth: that conditioned life is suffering. In receiving
a "new vision of his father," he intuitively grasps the second and
third Noble Truths: that suffering has a cause, and an end.

These metaphors of religion, myth, poetry, and art provide us
with the new dreams, the new visions of possibility, however idealistic or imaginary, that can give us the force we need to go forward.
Religion, myth, poetry, or literature can take the longing and the
absence we feel and transform it, not by glossing over it and pretending it isn't there, but by giving it energy and purpose, raising
it to another level so that we can see a way out of our doldrums.
For Simone Weil, the absence of "the father" is not a tragedy but
an infinite opportunity for transcendence. "God can only be present in creation under the form of absence," she writes. "Nothing
which exists is absolutely worthy of love. We must therefore love
that which does not exist."[3]

Present-day society doesn't offer us much in the way of vision.
Instead of vision we have consumption, in place of the journey we
have the mortgage. We are enjoined to go to well-lit, merchandise-
rich stores to shop for our true satisfaction, rather than to rum-
mage around for it in the obscure corners of the soul. And even
when we are offered religious comfort, more often than not it is in
the form of worn-out piety, or cut-and-dried doctrines of certainty
that close down our questioning and journeying, rather than providing us with spiritually challenging practices that might open us
up. To sail out onto the sea of stories, ride the inner waves of fear,
courage, and endurance, so that we can come home with some
sense of joy and grandeur, we need a vision more meaningful than
what the mundane, present world has to offer us.

I am inspired by the vision of the compassionate servant, a

person who finds a deep peace and satisfaction not in accomplishment or accumulation, or even in mystical transport, but rather
in wisdom gained through service to others, through friendship,
love, silence, and truth. All religions I know of offer this model.
Such a vision does not necessarily require that we be hermits,
monks, or saints, that we scorn the "things of the world" as evil
or decadent. Though this vision sometimes requires renunciation,
periods of time (for some, perhaps a whole lifetime) when we
naturally find that it is better to be quiet and to have nothing than
it is to run around in search of that elusive something we think we
need, the life of the compassionate servant can be a full life, a life
of joy, interest, and discovery.

In Buddhism the vision of the compassionate servant is imagined in the figure of the bodhisattva, literally an "enlightening
being," committed to bringing peace, happiness, and illumination
to all, certain that this is not only possible, but that it will definitely be achieved. The bodhisattva is naïve and enthusiastic, hard
to discourage, always kind to others, feeling their feelings and suffering their sufferings, sparing no effort, refusing no vows that
might lead to the final achievement of his or her impossible goal to
save everyone, eliminate all evil and delusion, master all spiritual
teachings, and in the end merge with all others to become nothing
but pure holy truth itself. Though utopian idealisms can be toxic,
the bodhisattva vision (and similar visions in other religious traditions) has the potential to do better than this, for it is grounded
in practical kindness, in the ethics of nonharming, flexibility, and
listening, and in the thoughtful consideration of what will really
work in this world as it is, not as it should be, to benefit others.
So the vision of the compassionate servant can be a healthy vision,
offering us immense scope for our living, without twisting us out
of shape as normal people.

One can't find one's way to a spiritual vision like this through
reading about it in books (though books might encourage us to
seek it) or wishing it were so. Like Telemachus, we need a little

help from our friends, and usually a certain amount of effort on our part. But if we have the help and make the effort, we can find a vision, and, finding it, can muster the courage to leave home as our ancestors, real and imagined, did before us. We too will set forth, prow pointed toward the dawn.

If you too are inspired by the vision of the compassionate servant and would like to try it on, here's a meditation you can practice.

Imagine you are surrounded by bodhisattvas, gentle, kind, energetic, helping figures, who are focused on you, and whose only purpose is to encourage you. These figures may take the form of people you actually know in your life, good friends or mentors, or they may take imaginative archetypal form, as Buddhas, or biblical figures, or admirable people from the past or present you would have liked to have had in your life. See them in your mind's eye all around you as you sit in your chair. Feel their support.

Now imagine greeting them one by one, offering them tea and sweets, flowers, gifts of various sorts to thank them for being there, and to ask them for further help as you try now to summon the best that's within you, so that you can endeavor to make the great commitment to devote yourself to others in kindness and compassion, as they have done. Be clear that this commitment is not one of self-sacrifice. Taking good care of yourself and taking care of others cannot be mutually exclusive. They depend on each other, for how could you care for others if you are not sound; and how could you ever become sound selfishly? For love and concern for others is the best way to nurture one's self. With this spirit, consider the following prayer from an eighth-century Indian text on the bodhisattva path:

May the naked now be clothed,
And the hungry eat their fill.
And may those parched with thirst receive
Pure waters and delicious drink.

May the poor and destitute find wealth,
The haggard and the careworn, joy.
May confidence relieve those in despair
And bring them steadfastness and every excellence.

May every being ailing with disease
Be freed at once from every malady.
May all the sickness that afflicts the living
Be instantly and permanently healed.

May those who go in dread have no more fear.
May captives be unchained and now set free.
And may the weak receive their strength.
May living beings help each other in kindness.

And as long as space endures,
As long as there are beings to be found,
May I continue likewise to remain
To drive away the sorrows of the world.[4]

Recite these verses slowly to yourself. If you can, memorize some of them, learning them "by heart," so they become your own. If you want, write your own verses, or just a single verse. Copy this verse onto a card and display it where you can see it every day. Recite it over and over again. In a gentle, simple, gradual, repetitive way, without being overly dramatic or inflated, take the spirit of these prayers into your feeling, thinking, and living.

7 / A Mentor's Path to Enlightenment

Gods and goddesses are important actors in ancient Greek myth. Unlike the God of the great monotheistic traditions, who is beyond all understanding and depiction and stands both within and beyond the world, the Greek gods are easily identifiable and locatable, and often contend with one another in ways that seem suspiciously human. The gods don't stay put at home on Mount Olympus. They constantly appear on earth to participate in the dramas of mortals, and each has his or her realm and role. Hermes delivers messages. Poseidon, Odysseus' great nemesis, is god of sea storms and earthquakes. And Athena, Odysseus' great ally, is goddess of cleverness and deception. Specializing in shape-shifting and disguise, Athena first appears as Mentes in order to inspire Telemachus, and later as a simulacrum of Telemachus himself so that she can gather recruits for the voyage while the actual Telemachus remains at home, within plain sight of the suitors. This deception is important, for the suitors do not want Telemachus to go forth in search of his father; Odysseus' absence and Telemachus' inaction suit them well. They would sooner kill him than let him go, which is why his journey outward must be secret. (When they do find out, too late, that he is gone, they plot his assassination.) When Telemachus finally sets sail under cover of darkness, telling no one, not even his mother, that he is going,

Athena accompanies him as Mentor, the trusted friend Odysseus had asked to watch over Telemachus until the boy came of age. As Mentor, Athena can protect and encourage Telemachus and his young sailors.

Mentor is of course the prototype for our idea of the mentor, an older, experienced person who acts as a stand-in for the parent, satisfying the need for parental support and approval without carrying all the potential for ambivalence and passion that the actual parent evokes. Any process of deep or lasting growth involves mentors; their effects on us are more mysterious and far-reaching than the practical aid or advice they provide. We learn from books, we learn from our senses, our thoughts, our emotions, our doing. We learn from what others tell us, and from what we overhear. Though mentoring may include several of these modes of learning, it is also essentially different, because the mentor's simple presence in our lives creates an alchemy that transfers a subtle inner power. This transference cannot happen in any other way. In addition to simple face time, body time—our sharing of time, space, and presence with a mentor—it involves the sharing of stories.

Athena has sent Telemachus forth on his voyage to search for such mentoring. He visits two important friends of his father, Nestor and Menelaus, who accompanied Odysseus to Troy and have important tales to tell. Nestor recounts the events immediately following the Trojan War. As soon as the war ended, he tells Telemachus, differences of opinion and hostility arose among the men. Agamemnon's faction felt it was essential that they make sacrifice to the gods before they could safely begin their homeward journey. A faction led by Menelaus, Agamemnon's brother, and including Nestor and Odysseus, felt that no sacrifice was necessary, and that the weary troops ought to head home as soon as possible. The two groups split up, each doing as it saw fit. Nestor recalls sailing with Odysseus, but here his story ends, for Odysseus, our "wily man of twisted ways," ambivalent about the right course to choose (here wiliness and cleverness is a disadvantage:

seeing too many possibilities, we become confused), suddenly swerves his ship around, heading, on second thought, back to join Agamemnon's camp. This is as much Nestor knows, as far as he can take the story. To find out more, Telemachus must journey to Menelaus' home.

Arriving at Lacedaemon, Telemachus at first conceals his identity from Menelaus, but reveals it inadvertently when tears well up in his eyes at the first mention of Odysseus. And when Telemachus' patrimony becomes obvious, Menelaus also breaks down crying, as memories of his dear friend Odysseus come flooding in on him. Now both of them are weeping, and the whole company starts to weep, giving themselves over fully to their grief, for none of them knows whether esteemed Odysseus lives or not.

Mentoring tales, whatever advice or counsel they may offer, are also always tales of grief. In a mentoring tale, an older person inevitably expresses, whether directly or indirectly, the fact that sorrow is always the past's legacy, simply because the past, whatever else it may be, is gone, never to be recovered. The mentoring tale also expresses the confidence that, despite this and no matter how regrettable it may have been, the past is instructive and survivable. The past fertilizes the present. Not a page of *The Odyssey* ever lets us forget the ten-years-long Trojan War, with all its slaughter, mayhem, and maiming, the many who went out, the few who returned after long trials on the treacherous sea. Likewise, any true history of any culture can never fail to reference the wars, disasters, and injustices that pervade its chronicles. Nor can the story of any life be without regret, shame, loss, and tragedy. Left to its own devices, youth looks ahead breathlessly to the future, without much appreciation for the bittersweet ambiguity of the past that has preceded and conditioned that future. Mentors evoke for us a flavor of what has come before, tempering our sense of anticipation and passion for what is still to come with a necessarily cautionary sense of what's gone by. To be truly aware of the human story—or our own story for that matter—is to be one step away from tears.

But sorrow can be overdone. Denial has a bad reputation, but I have always considered it one of humanity's great achievements. The capacity to forget the past sometimes and to go on with our story as if tomorrow were a brand-new, unadulterated, day, as if our bright hopes were actually reasonable, is a good and necessary thing. That we maintain our capacity to imagine a happily-ever-after world in the face of what has actually happened throughout human history is a tremendous achievement. Without this profoundly imaginative act the human race would long ago have given itself over to continual weeping. Without this glorious denial, no one would fall in love, have children, or create anything. As psychologists and religious people constantly tell us, we avoid the truth of the drastic nature of the human condition at our own peril. On the other hand, they also tell us that this avoidance is sometimes a virtue, for optimism is healthier than pessimism.

It's good that we can fool ourselves about our lives for as long as we need to. In my early twenties, after having done much reading about Zen, I met someone who had actually done Zen meditation and could teach me how to do it. I had never meditated before and was immediately struck by the spookiness of silence and of simply being with myself in such a naked way. It was as if, just sitting still for a few moments, I could see flashing before my eyes the abyss that awaited me when I gave myself fully to meditation practice. I say "when" and not "if," because it was also apparent to me that I was going to do meditation practice, and that I was going to devote my life to it. But not right away. I wasn't ready. I was only twenty-one or twenty-two years old, had a certain amount of running around and being crazy to do, and knew I needed to do that first, before I got around to meditation (which in fact I did, a few years later). So although I am fond of the urgent feeling of Rabbi Hillel's famous rhetorical question about the religious life, "If not now, when?" I am sympathetic to the answer "Later," which is quite different from, and a much better answer than *"Maybe later."* These days when I see students who are not quite able to be serious about their spiritual practice, starting and stopping it many times, I am, because of my own experience, sympathetic. I know they will get around to it some time, if not in this life then in the next.

This question of denial or deferral also reminds me of an incident that happened at a large conference of Buddhist meditation teachers and Catholic monastics I attended years ago. Pope John Paul II had recently issued some papal document that seemed to denigrate meditation practice, arguing that it was a narcissistic avoidance mechanism, a way of blissing out of this world, possibly a dangerous form of self-obsession or self-indulgence, like a drug. One of the Catholic brothers mentioned this view and challenged a Buddhist to defend meditation, so I immediately rose to speak about how meditation was not a drug; no, no, it was the opposite of a drug, it promoted mindfulness, clarity, clear truthful seeing, wisdom, knowledge, compassion . . . anyway, I went on in this vein. After I had spoken, Joseph Goldstein, the Western Buddhist pioneer, who happened to be my roommate for the conference, rose to differ. "What's wrong with a drug?" he began. "Don't we need a drug sometimes? To cure us when we are ill, to relieve our pain, to give us a break when the going gets tough?"

In any case, yes, we need all sorts of things, different things at different times, and in spiritual matters we need to be practical and flexible. Spiritual practice is nutrition for the soul, and you can neither cook nor eat while you are weeping. Cooking requires some happiness, and happiness may require letting things slide from time to time, so that we can get a little relief from the seriousness of our troubles. In *The Odyssey* it's interesting that Helen, whose beauty had been the cause of all this grief in the first place (for it was her abduction by the Trojan Paris from her husband Menelaus' household that precipitated the war), calms down the extravagant display of weeping by Menelaus and Telemachus. She slips a grief-dissolving potion into the men's wine, so that they can pull themselves together and get on with the royal dinner party. Under the influence of her drug, Menelaus eventually recovers his composure, and gets on with his tale.

Let's meditate on how to best digest the past.

Think of aspects of your past that have been difficult or disappointing. Imagine them as a lump or a ball inside you. Place the ball in your chest or your heart, or place it deep in the pit of your stomach. Sense the ball's weight, its density. Let it contain the whole of the difficult past. Allow it to be there. Breathe it in when you inhale; breathe it out when you exhale. Observe the feelings that arise in you as you do so. Is the weight of the past disturbing? Do tears come to your eyes? Do you feel regret? Fear? Anger? Maybe you don't have much feeling, just the physical weight, the bodily discomfort.

Let yourself be with the weight and any feelings until calmness comes upon you, as it surely will. Time will pass, and whatever it is you have been feeling will settle. There will just be the breathing, the being present with what is.

Now imagine the ball becoming lighter and brighter. Let it become, as you continue breathing, more and more light and bright, until it seems to float in you, and to come to rest as a bright glow suffusing the space inside, illuminating your whole body. Breathe for a while enjoying this.

The past isn't heavy or light, good or bad. It is all of this, and none of it. In order to go on with the journey home we need to see the past from all sides, dark side, light side. If possible, we need to develop an optimistic, open feeling in order to go forward. With some patience and some effort this can be done. Being willing simply to look at, be with what's inside, will always eventually bring an appreciative accepting feeling to ripeness within you.

It seems that Agamemnon was right: sacrifices to the gods were necessary. As punishment for having failed to make them, Menelaus is stranded for a long time off the coast of Egypt without a wind to move his ships. Days, weeks go by; stores run dry; there is nothing for the men to eat. Menelaus is desperate to discover which of the gods he's offended, and how to make things right. The ocean goddess Eidothea rises up dripping from the waves to offer advice. She tells Menelaus that he can get what he needs from Proteus, her father, the hoary Old Man of the Sea, whose nature is to be absolutely truthful and helpful and to fulfill all requests— providing you are persistent enough to keep hold of him. And this is no easy matter, for Proteus is a changeable god, full of transformative energy, hard to pin down. In fact, he has no set shape. (Proteus gives us our word *protean*, which means "of a continually changing nature.") When confronted, he will turn himself into all sorts of terrifying creatures in order to elude your grasp. So when you grab him, the goddess cautions, be ready for anything, and whatever you do, hold on.

Eidothea helps Menelaus craft a plan: now and then Proteus hauls out of the sea to rest in a shoreside cave, comfortable among his offspring, a litter of seal pups. He sleeps soundly there and it is there you can snatch him. Eidothea goes so far as to supply Menelaus and his men with some sealskins for disguise, but they are so stinky the men can't stand them, so Eidothea, ever the accommodating goddess, supplies a perfume to be applied under the nostrils.

Menelaus and his men, now perfectly and comfortably disguised, lie in wait among the seals for a long time. Finally Proteus comes ashore and, suspecting nothing, sinks into deep slumber. The desperate sailors make the grab, the wily god leaps up, and in short succession turns into a lion, a serpent, a leopard, a boar, a towering column of water, and a tall tree. But somehow the men manage to hold on, until eventually Proteus, exhausted and defeated, has to follow his truthful, helpful nature. He tells them how to sacrifice and where, and assures them of safe passage home if they will do as he advises. When Menelaus, greedy for more good news, asks for information about their comrades ("Who made it home? Who has died? Who's still shifting on the open seas?") Proteus tells all: how Ajax the Lesser insulted the gods and so went down into the sea, with all his men, to a watery grave; how Agamemnon, after much travail, made it home, only to be killed by Aegisthus, who stole his wife and his kingdom; and how the last of the great leaders, Odysseus, still lives, stranded on Ogygia, held captive there by the goddess Calypso.

And so old Menelaus, in recounting his own struggles, tells young Telemachus, at last, exactly what he needs to hear.

The story of Proteus tells us that we can escape from a tough situation by holding fast in the face of many quick and dangerous changes. This is the practice of forbearance, my favorite spiritual discipline. Though it is not very popular or exciting, forbearance is the greatest of all spiritual qualities, because without it all other good qualities, intentions, insights, and powers will be wiped away as soon as the first leopard, serpent, or boar appears in the vicinity. You can be strong, intelligent, kind, say your prayers every day, meditate till your legs fall off. You can have beautiful spiritual experiences, meet God face to face, serve your neighbor with compassion and zeal. You can be creative and talented in many ways. But if you are not ready and able to hang in there when conditions suddenly and fiercely change, then your spiritual practice, however devoted or brilliant it may be, is in the final analysis pretty useless. It's the changes, the constant shifts and sudden reversals, that prove us, so we ought to appreciate them, even look forward to them, unpleasant though they may be at times, for it is thanks to them that we are forced to develop forbearance.

The Chinese ideograph for forbearance is a heart with a sword dangling over it, another instance of language's brilliant way of showing us something surprising and important fossilized inside the meaning of a word. Vulnerability is built into our hearts, which can be sliced open at any moment by some sudden shift in the arrangements, some pain, some horror, some hurt. We all know and instinctively fear this, so we protect our hearts by covering them against exposure. But this doesn't work. Covering the heart binds and suffocates it until, like a wound that has been kept dressed for too long, the heart starts to fester and becomes fetid. Eventually, without air, the heart is all but killed off, and there's no feeling, no experiencing at all.

To practice forbearance is to appreciate and celebrate the heart's vulnerability, and to see that the slicing or piercing of the heart does not require defense; that the heart's vulnerability is a good thing, because wounds can make us more peaceful and more real—if, that is, we are willing to hang on to the leopard of our fear, the serpent of our grief, the boar of our shame without running away or being hurled off. Forbearance is simply holding on steadfastly with whatever it is that unexpectedly arises: not doing anything; not fixing anything (because doing and fixing can be a way to cover up the heart, to leap over the hurt and pain by occupying ourselves with schemes and plans to get rid of it). Just holding on for dear life. Holding on with what comes is what makes life dear.

Imagine you are swimming in the ocean. Suddenly strong waves begin to come in, one after another. At first you are frightened, you panic, you try to escape. But you can't possibly get to shore fast enough: there is no way to outswim the waves. You realize you are going to have to forbear, to swim with the waves or let them wash over you.

The best way to do this is to be calm, to feel your fear but not to let your body or mind become destabilized by it. To do this, concentrate on the sensations of your body and your breath. This will help you get hold of yourself. Then, observe the waves closely. Find their rhythm. Observe yourself closely. Now you can enter the waves and ride them forward. Their energy will carry you that much closer to shore.

Sometimes this doesn't work: a wave comes crashing down on your head. Even then, if you stay aware of yourself, and don't try to escape, it's okay. You are pulled under for a moment (this is a surprisingly peaceful experience), then you come bobbing up a little farther toward shore than you were before.

Sit in your chair imagining this, feeling the strength of the wave and the strength of your forbearance. See yourself arriving back on shore where, invigorated, you appreciate what has just happened.

A friend once told me of something that had happened to her that was so upsetting she was absolutely beside herself. She is a very moderate, kind individual, an experienced Buddhist practitioner, as are many of my friends—but what had happened was so terrible that she was amazed by the violence of her reaction. It was as if she were in some sort of emotional toxic shock. She had obscene, even murderous, thoughts. She felt it was dangerous for her to go out of the house or even to talk with anyone because she would be a danger to herself and those around her. So she stayed indoors for days, keeping a close watch on her mind, neither denying nor indulging her anger, holding on for dear life, weathering the storm. Eventually, her feelings died down. And here is the striking thing: after the anger left her she found that her ability to hear had been restored to her. For a long time she had been losing her hearing, and even when her hearing had been good it had never been very good. But now she could hear perfectly. All she wanted to do was to sit and listen to the sound of birds, or to music. Not having been musical before, she could now hear every note and appreciate every musical nuance. She was sure that the powerful emotion that had raged through her had somehow changed her whole system, giving her a power she'd never had before.

Simply holding on this way may sound passive. Forbearance has a bad reputation in our culture, whose conventional wisdom tells us that we ought to solve problems, fix what's broken, grab what we want, speak out, shake things up, make things happen. And should none of this work out, then we are told we ought to move on, take a new tack, start something else. But this line of thinking only makes sense when we are attempting to gain external satisfaction. It doesn't take into account internal well-being; nor does it engage the deeper questions of who you really are and what makes you truly happy, questions that no one can ignore for long. We don't have to be sages or philosophers to understand that what makes us happy is less what we have than what we are. And what we are is protean: changeable, constantly shifting, empty, and magnificent as a tall tree or a column of water—if we will allow it. Taking refuge in our changeability, in our inner transformative energy, is a better way to find happiness, a more valuable treasure than anything we could ever get from outside. Insofar as forbearance helps us to embrace this transformative energy and allow its magic to work on us, as it did with my friend's hearing, forbearance isn't passive at all. It's a powerfully active spiritual force.

Zen practice has a reputation for being strict and tough, probably because people have read too many Zen books—and this includes some Zen teachers who also might have read too many Zen books and so set up Zen centers that aspire to reproduce the Zen style written about in the books. The ancient Chinese monastics living in mountain monasteries may have had a taste for the rugged life, but the essence of what they taught and practiced transcends strictness and toughness.

Still, like life, Zen practice isn't too easy, either. In a way, a Zen retreat, with its long hours of silent sitting practice, is a controlled, benign catastrophe, guaranteed to produce the sorts of fierce, rapid changes that Proteus springs on Menelaus and his men. But a fierce Zen master and a strict meditation schedule are not required for the production of catastrophes. Life will do that for us quite naturally. Any moment is a catastrophe, a total disaster, a fierce and bracing challenge, if we are awake to it. Any moment calls forth forbearance.

In a Zen retreat we have a format for working with these quicksilver changes: we sit with them, we pay attention to them, but at the same time pay attention to the breath, the body, to sitting, walking, standing, washing dishes, and so on. Being steady with mindfulness as an anchor for all the changes we go through is the way we practice forbearance. And you can employ this same method anywhere and anytime: just pay close attention to the details of what is going on internally and externally. Don't flinch, don't run away. Trust what happens. Take your stand there.

What impresses me about the story of Buddha's quest for enlightenment is not his brilliance or his meditation power but his forbearance in the face of tremendously difficult changes. Religious founders are usually imagined as heroes or superior people, so we might naturally think that the Buddha was extraordinary, that his enlightenment was full of deep spiritual experiences, that he was in command throughout. But actually it was the opposite. The Buddha had a tremendously hard time on his night of enlightenment. All his desires, doubts, and fears, all his guilt and regret and shame came to him vividly and strongly. In the traditional story these appear as various demons and temptresses that flash up one after another, almost exactly like the transformations of Proteus, only even more devastating and terrifying. I think the Buddha must have been quite dismayed by all this, maybe even scared to death.

What saved the Buddha was his original commitment to practice forbearance. With as much equanimity as he could muster, he remained seated on his meditation cushion, patient with all the colorful things that arose. In the end, at his deepest point of extreme suffering, he held on for dear life, trusting his own body and the earth on which he sat to support him in his struggle. He gave himself over to the wisdom of his own flesh, fruit of the earth, and to the immediacy of his own body, his own life right where he was. In doing that, his mind quieted. And then his experience of enlightenment unfolded.

In other words, the Buddha didn't create his enlightenment or produce it. Like my friend's miraculous hearing restoration, it simply happened as a natural unfolding of holding on for dear life in the face of ultimate adversity. It happened just as effortlessly and as naturally as a star rising in the sky. Although in the story enlightenment is presented as a final moment of fulfillment (stories always need a beginning, some conflict, and, preferably, a happy ending), in fact the Buddha's enlightenment unfolded day by day for the rest of his life. Every day for the rest of his life he continued his practice of forbearance, hanging on for dear life through the various changes that occurred—his backaches and stomachaches, the various disputes and problems in his order, the regicides, wars, famines, deaths, his own aging—and so built on his enlightenment experience, understood it, expanded it, and deepened it every day. Even after the Buddha's life ended, the experience of his enlightenment persisted. It went on in the forbearance of the people with whom he had lived and practiced, who developed the Buddha's awakening still further. And anyone who practices true forbearance, staying steady with life through its changes and catastrophes, holding on and not running away, will also bear witness to the ongoing unfolding of the Buddha's enlightenment.

8 / Practice with the Body

Note that the basis of the Buddha's forbearance, and the basis of ours as well, is the body. When things get tough in Zen practice, we hold on with the body, paying close attention to the body in sitting, walking, breathing, and so on. Staying with the body brings calm, and gives us a concrete, definite way to be with our experience without running away.

In the Abhidharma, the Buddhist psychological teachings, the body is called "the soil in which understanding grows." This is of course true: the body calms and grounds the mind and heart, and a stable mind and heart produce wisdom and happiness. And yet (another paradox!) the trustworthy body is also, like the heart, radically vulnerable. In fact, this is its very nature. The Abhidharma's definition of the body is "that which can be molested." In other words, the nature of the body—and of everything that is material, physical—is that it can be broken, squashed, scraped, scratched, burned, and worn away. Thoughts and feelings may be pleasant or unpleasant, but they cannot be broken, squashed, burned, or worn away. How is it that this fundamentally breakable body is the basis of truth, enlightenment, redemption? What is it about the body that makes it the ideal vehicle for our journey of return?

•　•　•

When I look in the mirror I see a familiar image I call myself. Once the image of an infant, then a child, then an adolescent, it now reflects a grown adult. Is it accurate to think of this series of images as one evolving person? Or, since science tells me that not a single cell that existed in my body at infancy exists in it now, is it more accurate to see this present image as someone new?

The human body is not an object in the world. It is a magnificent process, a ceaseless flow, a journey in itself. Without my intending or thinking about it, my heart beats, my lungs expand and contract, blood surges through many thousands of miles of capillaries, arteries, and veins, nourishing muscles and organs. When the sense organs receive stimulation, a world springs into view as chemical and electrical reactions in the brain and nervous system give rise to thoughts, emotions, intentions, experiences. Without making any complicated or belabored effort, I can naturally desire, move, act in this world.

I eat a meal but I don't digest—the body does this on its own, whether I want to or not, taking meat and bread, eggs, fish, and carrots, and transforming them into energy and waste, into meaning, purpose, dilemmas, love. They're transformed into life, the ongoing flow of life that expresses itself through the body I call "me," as if I owned it, as if I knew what it was, as if I were in charge of it, and could direct it according to my will. What is my will exactly? In what part of my body does it reside?

I can tell my body to walk or sit or stand or jump, and it will. But I cannot order my body not to age or not to bleed if my finger is cut. If I become ill I can tell my body to get well, but I do not know if it will obey. My body will fight the illness whether I tell it to or not, and most of the time my body will eliminate the illness, restoring itself to health, because no matter how sick my body becomes, there is always more right with it than wrong. The body is a vehicle for life's flow; it is ruled by life, determined by life, much more than it is ruled and determined by me.

I did not design nor engineer this body, nor did I choose it, ordering it from a selection of floor models. Somehow the body appeared without the application of volition on my part, and then later on, little by little, "I" began to inhabit the body, although I am not sure I can say that "I" am something other than the body. I can't imagine what "I" would be without the body, yet I can think of myself as other than the body, as thought, as feeling, as a vague sense of subjectivity I take quite for granted though I can neither define nor completely confirm its existence. All my desire, intention, will, effort, emotion, and intelligence, are very small and crude, compared to the body's skills—the mystery, power, and subtlety of the body's ongoing flow.

The body does not persist endlessly on its course. When the flow of life, having passed through the body for just the right amount of time, moves on, the body becomes inanimate, a mere physical presence, uncanny still, but in a different way. Like all physical objects, the inanimate body dissolves gradually into the elements that make it up. What will I be when that happens? But even after the body dissolves into air, water, fire, earth, and light, life will still flow on. My thinking, my desire, my language, my sense of vulnerability, my conditioning, sees the breakup of the body as my tragic problem. But the body does not have this problem. For all I know, the body might see its final dissolution as an exciting journey of return, a liberation, a homecoming, a release, a frolic through time, space, and beyond.

The living body breathes. This is one of its most salient features. Air enters through nostrils or mouth, fills the lungs, enriches the blood that flows through the heart and from the heart throughout the body, renewing life. Then, easily and naturally—without any decision or intention on my part—spent air goes out through mouth or nostrils, carrying with it what the body no longer needs, releasing the body's past, its used-up moments, out into the world from which they came. Moment after moment the body does this: renewing life, letting go of life, with each breath in and out. Breathing is another version of the journey of return.

A sudden breath is the first thing that happens when the tiny mammalian body leaves its watery home inside its mother and enters the harsh, cold light of the outer, wider world. The first breath in, rush of cold air: what a shock! How unexpected, how unwelcome. The first breath must feel sharp, aggressive, like the world forcing us to participate whether we want to or not, causing us to gasp, as we will continue to gasp for the rest of our lives in the face of life's relentless aggression. We cry out, though none of us remembers this. And at the end of a life, when the final moment comes, the moment when the body returns home to earth, its elements seeking their original places of repose ("Dust to dust, ashes to ashes"), the lungs let go and there is one last breath out. And there is peace, rest, rejoining.

Human life in the world always begins with an inhalation and always ends with an exhalation. And between those two decisive breaths there is always breathing going on. We say "we breathe," but it would be better to say "we are breathed." Twenty-four hours a day, three hundred sixty-five days a year, year after year, decade after decade, there is no end, no pause, to breathing. If, out of disgust for life, or out of sheer weariness, we wanted to stop breathing, we could not. All our will power, all our despair, fear or loathing would not be sufficient to carry out the intention "from now on I will not breathe."

There is only so much air on the planet, and we must share it with all other breathing creatures. Now, and since the beginning of breathing, we have all been breathing the same air, taking it into our bodies, transforming it and being transformed by it, using it to move through time, moment by moment, to be what we are. This is intimacy: we take into our bodies the very air that others have breathed. Molecules of air that Buddha breathed, that Jesus breathed, that Plato, Hitler, Napoleon, Einstein, Shakespeare, the pope, the heavyweight champion of the world breathed; air breathed by men, women, and children, by heroes and murderers, by animals, plants, and insects, throughout time on Earth—some of these same molecules have been inside of us.

In the Bible's great story of creation, God creates the mountains, the sky, the sea, and all that dwells within them by pronouncing words. But the human being is created when God breathes a breath into him. One of the Hebrew words for soul, *nefesh* (and also the Greek word, *pneuma,* the Latin word, *spiritus*), means breath. Soul, spirit is breath.

For some years before his enlightenment night Buddha tried all sorts of extreme practices. He meditated on bliss, peace, and happiness. When this did not produce the lasting change he sought, he meditated on spaciousness, consciousness, nothingness, and on a state called neither-perception-nor-nonperception. When none of these profound trances helped, he tried ascetic practices. He stood on one foot in a lake with water up to his neck for days at a time. He tried cow practice and dog practice—not speaking or bathing, and eating, sleeping, behaving, and vocalizing as if he were a cow or a dog. Next he tried hardly eating at all, till gradually he got down to one sesame seed a day. When none of these worked, he gave them up, too.

On the point of despair, the Buddha suddenly remembered a simple natural meditation that he'd fallen into when he was a child sitting under an apple tree at a festival, just quietly breathing, just being aware. So he decided to trust the feeling of his childhood, and to return to this simple practice, which, as he sat under the enlightenment tree, finally won him through to awakening. Zen meditation is just this simple, childish practice. Just sitting, just breathing, being with whatever arises, but then letting go and coming back to just sitting and breathing, trusting that being alive in the body, the breath, the mind, and the heart is enough. Being content not to know, but simply to be present with life as it appears.

Meditation is not what we think it is: it is not peacefulness or bliss or even a technique for insight or enlightenment. Meditation is simply creating the space within us that will allow our lives (without defining too much, without desiring too much) to engage the states of being about which I have been writing: waiting for nothing, ripening our feelings so that we can speak them when the time comes, leaving home, returning home. In meditation these things can be very real. They can occur naturally, without forcing or preconceiving anything. In this widest sense, meditation is an open and creative way of returning home to ourselves, a way in which the mystery that we actually are can have its full expression. Meditation is not limited to a particular technique or posture: any open-ended spiritual or creative exercise can be a form of meditation.

Formal sitting meditation practice, as done in Zen or other schools of Buddhism (and in other traditions, too), is a powerful way to foster this open, creative engagement with ourselves. In formal sitting we practice the journey of return in a literal way, returning awareness to the breath, to the body, to the present moment, whenever it strays away. Most simply understood, formal sitting meditation is the effort to return to the concrete feeling of being alive, a feeling that is always with us, but that we almost never notice, so preoccupied are we with our problems and issues. Meditation in general, and formal sitting meditation in particular, is radically simple. There's almost nothing to it. Letting go, coming back: that's all. The only difference between meditation and non-meditation is that when we meditate we are not grasping anything or trying to do anything: instead we are releasing ourselves to our lives, with trust that our lives are all we need. A monk once asked Zen Master Zhaozho what meditation is. "It's nonmeditation," he answered. "How can meditation be nonmeditation?" the monk said. "It's alive!" was Zhaozho's response.

Here is a simple formal meditation practice I often teach. Like all meditation techniques it is provisional, which is to say, it is not crucial that you do it precisely or correctly or that you take it too seriously. The point of it is to help you in your effort to return to the present, which can some-
 ; be difficult without something concrete to focus on.

First, sit down in a quiet spot. Whether you sit on a chair
or a cushion, sit up straight, with your spine extended, your
upper body open. Fold your hands in your lap, put them on
your knees, or use the Zen hand position of left palm on
top of right, with the palms gently curved, making an oval,
thumb tips just barely touching. Cast your eyes downward
(you can close them if you like, but watch out not to get too
dreamy or sleepy) and begin by sweeping your awareness
lightly through the body: forehead, eyes, cheeks, jaw, neck,
shoulders, arms, and so on. The point is to arrive in the
body, to be aware of the body as sensation and process, to
ground yourself in the body as basis so that thought and
emotion don't fly too far afield.

Once you are actually sitting there, all of you, mind
and body in one place, begin to turn your attention to the
breath. Breathe in and out gently through the nose, paying
attention to the breath in the abdomen area. Begin with
counting the breath, saying the numbers silently, one to
ten, with each exhale. If you lose count, go back to one and
begin again, as much as possible without blame or dismay.
Once you can count fairly well, or get bored with counting,
next just follow the breath in the belly, feeling it there, in,
out, in, out, and so on (you can say these words, or, better, just be with the sensation, or, still better, be the sensation).

If this begins to make you sleepy, or if you would just
like to move on, see the whole breath more brightly and
fully: become aware of the beginning, middle, and end of
the inhalation; the beginning middle and end of the exhalation; the odd and almost imperceptible places where inhalation ends and exhalation begins; or exhalation ends and
inhalation (after a nonbreathing gap) begins. Every breath
is a whole life: see if you can feel that life and live it fully,
from one end of it to the other.

If you can, and would like to, move on, then make the
breath vivid and alive, brighter and brighter, as if you were
turning up a rheostat to make the light in your room gradu-

ally brighter. Now you don't need to count, follow, or see the whole breath—just make it alive, breath after breath, until it is full of interest and passion. If you can get that far, then you will be able to let go of the breath altogether and just sit with an open awareness, open to sounds, thoughts, feelings, the whole universe that swirls around you and inside you.

To summarize the process: establish awareness of the body; count; follow; discriminate the whole breath; make it alive; jump off. These are the steps, but it is not necessary to do them all, or to do them in this order. Be flexible with your practice and figure out for yourself what is most natural, what will work to give you a grounding strong enough to bring you back to the present moment of your being alive right here where you are. Also, remember to stay engaged with the feeling of the body the whole time, which you will find that you can do, even while you are paying attention to the breath. After twenty to thirty (or more!) minutes of meditation, if you have time, you may find it worthwhile to spend another fifteen minutes doing some spiritual reading, or some prayer, chanting, or other exercise or form of worship.

—☙—

Repetition is the soul of spiritual practice. In any tradition I know of, there are daily practices like this one, and a sense of faithfulness to a daily routine. This takes some gentle self-discipline, encouraged by some support from others within whatever spiritual community you can find to belong to. Doing the same thing over and over again may seem dull, but the more you immerse yourself in spiritual practice, diving into it day after day like jumping into the bracing ocean with its sunlit wavetips, the more wonderful it becomes. Life's like that, too. We might seek novelty, but even where there seems to be novelty, what's really going on underneath the surface is pattern repetition. Whether we are in Hawaii on vacation, sick in the hospital, or absorbed in our workweek, there is always going to sleep, waking up, eating, going to the toilet, walking, standing, sitting, reclining, seeing, hearing, tasting, touching, smelling, feeling, thinking. Every day goes this way. The sun rises, the sun sets. Life comes, goes, and comes back again. You could see this as boring. Or you could realize that life's archetypal repetition is a form of the journey of return, the deep joy of moment-by-moment renewal, with each breath and heartbeat. The daily routine of spiritual practices brings this reality home to us. Gertrude Stein, the great genius of repetition, once said, "The question of repetition is very important. It is important because there is no such thing as repetition." Each moment in the ever-repeated pattern is, by virtue of the repetition, always new; whatever comes back around again in the great cycle of things is always fresh.

The journey of return is profound, but it is also vague and dark. It is, to a great extent, hidden from us. And yet we know about it. The world's religious and imaginative literature gives us many hints and pointers, and we ourselves have inklings and flashes of it at the center of our experience and sometimes at the edges. So we know it is real and we know how much it matters. The journey of return involves not only our so-called "spiritual lives" but the whole of our lives, our work, relationships, creative expression, dreams, sickness, wellness, and dying. Meditation practice is at the center of the journey of return, fueling and inspiring us.

Return goes on no matter what you do, whether you intentionally or formally engage in spiritual practice or not. But when you meditate, pray, sing, dance, or whatever it is you do repeatedly, for no reason other than an Odysseus-like faithfulness to your journey home, you begin to notice how strange and mysterious life is. When your spiritual practice is regular, you don't forget about that mystery as easily as you otherwise might, when life's exciting stories cart you off again and again on distracting adventures, only to disappoint you in the end, leaving you spent and dazed.

Spiritual practice in all its manifestations is the practice of coming home. If we struggle in our spiritual exercises, as we so often do, it's not because they are too difficult or we are poor practitioners. It's because our many journeys outward and our many tricks and deceptions have left us twisted and turned around, and it takes some struggle before we can relax into our real shape. Struggle is a part of the journey, and, as Odysseus will find out soon enough, there will inevitably be disasters as we go onward, because the gods have decided in advance to give us the trouble we need.

Part Two

Disaster

Unavoidably, disaster teaches us lessons we thought we'd learned

Then, if you keep your mind on homecoming,
and leave these unharmed,
you might all make your way to Ithaka, after
much suffering.

 —*The Odyssey*[1]

9 / Working with Disaster, Pleasure, and Time

The spiritual process reveals the contours of a life story, its peaks and valleys. Whether or not we tell our story, the stark truth of our lives always appears in the way we are to anyone who has the eyes to see. Bearing witness to so many stories over the years, I have come to appreciate life's tremendous range of weird and challenging experiences, of its joys, delights, amazements . . . and disasters. No life, even the greatest and most fortunate, is without its disasters, which make the story interesting.

We've been trained to avoid disasters, to believe that, if we were really good, really smart, really energetic, really mindful, disasters would not occur, and that therefore when they do, it must be because there is something wrong with us. We must have made some mistake. But that's not so. Disasters can't be avoided. Sometimes the disaster is indeed due to a fault or miscalculation of ours. Sometimes disaster occurs because of someone else's intentional or unintentional action. And sometimes disaster just happens, with no rhyme or reason to it. But it makes no difference. Human imperfection is not a mistake, it is normal. Character is fate. The disasters that befall us are the disasters we need in order to advance the plot of the story we are living. Still, when disaster strikes, we feel devastated, ashamed, and chagrined. "This should never have happened," we say. And when we recover from our shock and dismay, we do as we've been trained to do: pick ourselves up and try to restore things to the state they were in before the disaster struck, with new provisions and declarations for safety and security, to ensure that such things will never again happen in the future.

We try to make the disaster disappear as quickly as possible (even if that requires us to ignore as much of it as is feasible) so that we can "get on with our lives," as if this unfortunate and altogether unacceptable interlude had never occurred. When the disaster is so powerful that we can't simply take it in stride, when it's so glaring that we're forced to remember and take it into account in our subsequent living, we then can fall back on a set of tried-and-true scenarios that will explain it away, making us sound like noble victims who have suffered and overcome, or contrite penitents who have learned their lesson. Usually, however, these scenarios are not true, but rather are false tales piled on top of false tales—customary strategies to tame, neutralize, deny what has happened even as we are apparently admitting it.

Disaster is a deeply engrained feature of life and of time. It is natural and useful, even though we don't like it. Although we think that happiness is the avoidance of disaster, in fact to be happy we need to recognize and appreciate disaster. To be happy in a meaningful way is to know how to face disaster and how to integrate it into our lives. To do this we must be able to feel the full force of disaster without flinching, and be able to digest it without being so profoundly scarred by it that our living from then on is distorted. For none of us will ever advance beyond all disaster. No matter where we are in life, disaster is always possible. This ought to make us humble, and at bottom, quiet and ready for the next turn of the narrative, whatever it may be. One of disaster's most disastrous features is that it always surprises us.

In part two of this book, we will consider *The Odyssey*'s most famous episodes, the so-called "wanderings of Odysseus," episodes we all know about whether we have read the poem or not. For these stories are part of the fabric of our culture, deeply embedded themes that pop up in movies, in novels, in our own life stories, and in the stories of our friends. All these famous episodes share a single characteristic: they are all disastrous. They are harrowing, tense, sometimes brutal, tragic, always colorful and instructive. Sometimes *The Odyssey's* disasters happen because Odysseus is arrogant, blind, or lazy, sometimes because his men are willful, greedy, cowardly or rebellious. And sometimes they happen simply because the gods will that they do.

All these things can be said about our disasters too. By reflecting on Odysseus' disasters we may be in a better position to accept the inevitability of our own, and to see how much we need disaster, and how to make use of it. For there is no journey home without trial and tribulation. Life itself, time itself is fundamentally disastrous. If we can take a deep breath and admit this glorious, frightening fact, we will be better off.

We left Odysseus stranded on Ogygia. There he lives as a captive of the goddess Calypso, who pampers him, believing that eventually her beauty and the luxury of the island life will wear him down, and he will fall in love with her and choose to remain there for the rest of his life. As we saw, however, Athena advocated for Odysseus at the council of the gods. She was successful in convincing Zeus that Odysseus should be set free. Zeus sent Hermes across the wide ocean to deliver the decree, which Calypso reluctantly passed on to her captive, as he sat in his usual spot weeping and gazing out to sea. At first Odysseus doesn't believe Calypso is sincere; he makes her vow that this is not a trick (being tricky himself, Odysseus is always suspicious). She does so, but issues one final plea: Ogygia is a lovely place. She is a permanently beautiful goddess. Why does Odysseus insist on taking a dangerous journey home to reunite with a mortal aging wife, an ambivalent angry son, and a troubled household, when instead he could enjoy all this, and immortality too?

"But even so," Odysseus tells her,

what I want and all my days I pine for
is to go back to my house and see my day of homecoming.
And if some god batters me far out on the wine-blue water,
I will endure it, keeping a stubborn spirit inside me,
for already I have suffered much and done much hard work
on the waves and in the fighting. So let this adventure follow.[1]

With this expression of commitment and willingness to face whatever comes, Odysseus begins the work of building a seaworthy craft.

Although from time to time Odysseus falls prey to discouragement or forgetfulness, throughout his journey he always comes back to his commitment to return home no matter what it takes. This faithfulness to his goal and his determination to endure anything to accomplish it are his chief motivations. But why is Odysseus so determined to go home, even now, when he has such a pleasant alternative on offer? And why are we willing to give up pleasant circumstances to bear the difficulties of the homeward journey?

In the traditional Buddhist and Indian journey of transmigration from one lifetime to the next, there are six realms of existence into which we are born: hell realm, fighting demon realm, and the realms of hungry ghosts, animals, humans, and gods. After death, a being enters the realm appropriate to his karma, spends the appointed amount of time there, accrues more karma, and moves on. One would think that among the options available, the god realm would be the most desirable, if not the ultimate destination. But this is not so. Yes, the realm of the gods is pleasant (nourishment is taken through the olfactory organ, so there is no messy sewage issue; sex can be indulged in mentally, removing any possible obstacle or discomfort). But it is too seductive, and its easy pleasures mask a tragedy. For behind the hazy smoke screen of enjoyment and delight that characterizes the god realm, a particularly noxious form of suffering is going on, a form of suffering that does not involve pain or unpleasantness, and which is therefore more insidious than the usual kind. The pleasures of the god realm hide the fact that a fall is inevitable, that sooner or later a god tumbles out of heaven only to land in a place that, by contrast, seems more terrible than it actually is, a place where he or she will have very little coping skill. In heaven, where there is no overt suffering, and where the pleasures are all-consuming, the gods have no incentive whatsoever to take steps to prepare for this fall, and so, through inaction, matters are made worse.

Odysseus understands this problem intuitively: the gods are trapped by their godliness. Humans, though seemingly less powerful and less happy, are better off. Our hearts know this, too. Just as we are born with self-awareness and intelligence, we are born knowing that the journey home, though arduous, is what we really need, and that there is no way to avoid it through some form of pleasant forgetfulness. For us, pleasure, ease, and enjoyment are nice enough, but insufficient. The gods may be happy as they are, but we need more reality than they can stand. No matter how gritty and dirty it may be from time to time, for us only reality will suffice, and reality propels us forward into our lives, come what may. Though we may go to great lengths to avoid pain and trouble whenever we can, the truth is that deep down we all welcome it if it must come, if that is what it takes to keep our lives real. We all hold to some values that are more dear than our own comfort.

When I began my spiritual practice long ago, this was my instinctive feeling. My goal was neither colorful exotic experiences nor a way to make my life enjoyable or smooth. I enjoyed fun as much as the next person. I was not an ascetic (though I came to discover that asceticism also has its pleasures), but I was driven to know and experience my life as it really was, as deeply as I could, and I was firmly convinced that this was the only worthy goal. I realized that sacrificing security and worldly accomplishment for something as vague as this was not going to be easy, and that the life I was after might not be pleasant—in fact, it would probably cause me a lot of trouble—but at least it would be real, and real is what I needed and wanted. I was willing to accept whatever difficulties arose as a consequence.

When it comes to determination to forgo comfort or pleasure in the quest for truth, it is hard to equal the ancient Christian hermits, the famous "desert fathers" whose love of God and zeal for truth knew no bounds. Though I, like most people, am fairly normal in my habits, and do not yearn to suffer in imitation of Jesus as many Christians throughout the ages have done, I can't help but admire the courage and singleness of purpose of these early saints. Saint Anthony is the original desert father, whose fierce asceticism set the model for this important early Christian movement. So intent was he on discovery of truth that he was said to be willing to travel anywhere at any time to seek out people of wisdom, and he would remain with them till "like a wise bee" he'd drunk deeply of the nectar of their teachings. For more than twenty years Anthony did solitary battle with demons, going to more and more remote and forbidding locales as the intensity of his struggles progressed. When this phase of his journey dramatically came to a close he complained to God, "Where were you? Why didn't you appear at the beginning to stop my pain?" And a voice said to him, "I was with you all along." After this time he emerged from his cave at the urging of his many friends, who found him to be, quite astonishingly, a modest, wise, and exacting teacher.[2]

In the end, no matter how ordinary or extraordinary we are in our way of life, we all require reality, truth, values, and commitments beyond the everyday pleasures and comforts. Nothing less will do. Whether we know it or not, or like it or not, we are built that way. It doesn't occur to animals, fighting demons, hungry ghosts, hell dwellers or gods to ask whether their lives are real or their values are true, because their lives are simply what they are, there's no choice involved, and they react according to their fates. But a human life can be real or it can be unreal, its basis true or untrue, depending on how we live, the choices we make. To live an unreal, trivial, or false life is the worst fate that can befall us. Though we may be tempted to stay for a while on Ogygia, maybe even a long while, like Odysseus, ultimately we would choose to leave. We all want to go home to our real life, because we know that's where we belong.

Imagine that, like the Buddha, like Odysseus, like Anthony, you too have a journey to take, a destiny to fulfill, a true home to return to. Maybe you don't do battle with demons or wrestle with shape-shifting gods, as they did, but your journey will be real. Take a few minutes to settle with your breath and with your body till you can feel this. Breathe, relax, come to quiet in your mind.

You may not know your way home yet, but you do know that you must find what's true and real for your life. You must make contact with the deeper impulse that's always stood behind the choices you have made, though you may not have known it at the time. Feel now the conviction that this impulse will grow within you as you sit quietly. Let the trivial and superficial veneer of your life slowly peel away, layer by layer, as you begin to feel the reality behind it, the true purposes for which you were born. Though you may have settled responsibilities, and a life for and with others that demands your attention (so that you can't, and wouldn't want to, run off to the desert or the sea), make up your mind that from now on you will use the details and tasks of your life for these higher purposes.

If there is something outwardly in your life that should be changed, have the courage to change it. If not, change the meaning, the feeling, in what you do. Determine to make your life real.

With such determination, and the inner preparations you made in part one, the journey begins. But of course your journey has already begun. When I ask people who have practiced Zen with me for a while to give talks about their personal spiritual journeys, they invariably begin somewhere in early childhood.

Beginning Zen practice and continuing with it for a while usually makes them realize that in fact their spiritual journey started long before they ever set foot in a Zen meditation hall, long before they ever thought of spiritual practice as something they wanted to take up. The journey has many beginnings, or none: the more you go on the more you see that you have been on this journey as long as you can remember, and even before that. This déjà vu sense of the spiritual journey of return is one of its salient features, and this feature is mirrored in the narrative structure of *The Odyssey*.

You may already have noticed that the sequencing of *The Odyssey's* events is rather convoluted. It begins on Ogygia, then immediately backs up so that we can hear about Telemachus, whose story involves a flashback to the days of Troy, ten years before any of the events of *The Odyssey* have taken place. Now we are back on Ogygia, which is not actually the beginning of Odysseus' story, but about three-fourths of the way through. From Ogygia, Odysseus sails to the land of the Phaiakians where, for five full books, he tells the earlier story of his wanderings, beginning with the departure from Troy and bringing us up to the time he is captured by Calypso (this long flashback contains most of the familiar Odyssean disasters, to which we will soon turn). His long story ended, Odysseus sails from the land of the Phaiakians home to Ithaca, where he is to face still more challenges (we'll hear about these in part three).

With this rather disorienting sequence of events, *The Odyssey's* sense of time is oddly fractured. In reading the poem, one is never quite sure where one is in time: whether in the past, which is shedding light on the present, or in the present, which reveals the meaning of the past, or, for that matter, in the future, whose events are often alluded to in the present or past. The "now" of *The Odyssey* is an ever-shifting affair, constantly deranging our sense of where we are in time. It is as if the poem, in charting Odysseus' forward progress in such a deliberately mixed-up way, is trying to tell us something about how we experience time along the course of our journey of return.

Time is not exactly what we think it is. This can be viscerally appreciated in a meditation retreat, when there is nothing to do, day after day, but sit in meditation, in silence, following a schedule that is repetitive not only from day to day but also from morning to afternoon to evening. Every period of meditation seems, after a while, timeless, sometimes lasting an eternity and sometimes seeming to end before it began. And as the days of the retreat wear on, you feel the sense of déjà vu I keep mentioning as your usual ways of marking time and experiencing it fall away and you begin to respond instead to the sounds of the temple bell and wooden sounding board. Your sense of time expands and contracts with an uncanny flexibility, until you cannot say whether time is passing very quickly or very slowly. Life seems almost a dream.

Years ago one of my Zen teachers decided to experiment a little with the feeling of time. He told the timekeeper during a long retreat not to strike the bell at the scheduled end of the period of meditation but instead to let the period go on until he gave the signal to end it. In that retreat there were some periods of meditation that lasted for over an hour and others that lasted for a few minutes (that is, by clock time). No one would know in advance whether the next meditation period was going to be a long one or a short one. Eventually we all saw that we had to sit down at the beginning of every period with no notion of time at all, no hope and no expectation, willing to stay there forever if need be ("let the adventure begin!"). Within a few days it was hard to be entirely sure of the difference between a long period and a short one. We had our impressions, but watches were not allowed. The experiment continued right up until the end of the retreat, which (no surprise by now to anyone) did not end at the scheduled time, but went on long into the night. It was an effective, dramatic experiment, but, by popular demand, was never repeated.

Even when periods of meditation are exactly as long as advertised, you can still experience this sense of time's thickness and uncanniness. You can experience it at other times, too, such as a birth or a death, or when you first hear powerfully good or bad news. At such moments time seems to be swept away entirely; a black hole opens and swallows it. This is not an illusion. Time is not nearly as well organized as we think it is; it really does have these odd gaps and chunks. Time doesn't flow neatly along a smooth continuum or horizontal "time line," with the past at the far left (since our Indo-European language reads from left to right) running to the present in the center and future at the far right. We take time for granted as a neat, even, neutral, constant container for our experiences. But this perception isn't correct or real. Time slows, speeds, or stops, according to the flow of your life. The view of time that you are conditioned to, in which your subjective sense of time is subservient to what the clock or calendar says, is a fairly recent invention. Time is not what clocks measure; time is what we experience as life, and as such it belongs more to the realm of the mysterious and the sacred than to the world of science and measurement.

Mystics from all spiritual traditions know this. They point out that God, Enlightenment, Oneness, or whatever you call it, which is both in time and beyond time, is encountered in the gap moments when time opens up in a transport that contains past present and future all at once or none of these. They also point out that sequential time is everywhere subject to divine violation, the past sometimes arriving lively and dripping into the present, the future from time to time bleeding into the past. "Time is not a storm moving across the sky from East to West," Zen Master Dogen writes. "Time is being itself."

So we go from life to death, but the reverse is also possible: in our experience of the thickness of time in the present, we may encounter a feeling of the presence of someone who has died, so that the person actually appears to us, in a palpable if not an entirely physical sense. And we can relive and clarify the past in the present, as anyone who has ever experienced lucid dreaming or psychotherapeutic insight knows. We can disappear from the present into the future in reverie. And we can connect in the present to any time, which will become thicker and more emotional as our hearts open to it. When we commit ourselves to the spiritual journey wholeheartedly, we throw ourselves into time in a different way. We don't forget about clock time, but we recognize it as the convention that it is, and we are always ready to be surprised. When you have a daily spiritual practice, you may often experience your life in time in ways that violate the conventional. The gods don't know about this.

For the great Jewish theologian Abraham Joshua Heschel, time was experiential evidence of God's presence. Human beings can conquer the physical world, the world of space, he wrote; they can improve or destroy it, smash it down, build it up (remember the Abhidharma definition of matter as "that which can be molested"). But human beings are utterly powerless to manipulate time. They can only live it, and be lived by it. "Time is the presence of God in the world of space," he writes, "and it is within time that we are able to sense the unity of all beings. . . . Time is this present moment because God is present. Every instant is an act of creation. A moment is not a terminal but a flash, a sign of Beginning. Time is perpetual innovation . . ."[3]

Inner growth and development require that we occasionally have this unconventional experience of time. Instinctively we know how much we need it. We seek it on long relaxing vacations, in the quiet of nature, in foreign countries; some people, less profitably, seek it in drugs, alcohol, or other forms of time derangement. The unconventional experience of time comes in retreats and in daily spiritual exercises, but it can also come on a more everyday basis simply by paying attention to what we are doing. Paying attention, being present seems normal and ordinary but it's not. Our usual everyday attention is quite dull. Watching the clock, we are half present, half aware. We are where we are but only partly; the rest of us is elsewhere, we don't know where, unconscious, muffled. When we really pay attention to where we are, the world brightens up a bit. Inner and outer things sharpen and are augmented in our basic sense of their being there.

No fancy or elaborate technique is necessary for paying close attention like this. All it takes is reminding yourself to be engaged with whatever is going on, to be actually and more fully here with it. When you slow down and apply awareness right where you are—to your acts of perception and volition, to speech, thought, and feeling (hearing when you hear, speaking when you speak, walking when you walk, eating when you eat, exactly as the old Zen masters taught)—you begin little by little to live within time's sacredness. In this way, simple awareness practice, which uses whatever is happening at the moment as its support and object, can be like the boat Odysseus is fashioning right now, bare poles lashed together with rope and pitch, that will carry him back out to sea, along his journey home.

Imagine being so present with your life, in any moment of time, that you can feel the presence of all of time in that moment. So present that mundane time falls away, and you feel time's sacredness.

You can do this now. Breathe. Breathe completely and fully, one complete full inhalation, one complete full exhalation. Feel each breath as it rises up from your belly to your lungs and heart, your nostrils, and then gently falls from nostrils to lungs to heart to belly. Be completely lost in each inhalation and exhalation, so long, so full, so sweet.

Now as you breathe, feel your body sitting in your chair. Feel the support of the chair. Feel gravity's steady subtle pull on you. Feel the blood circulating, the heart beating. Feel sensations: hardness of your teeth, softness of your lips, the tiny muscles around the eyes, coolness of forehead, warmth of armpits.

Expand your awareness. Sense the space around you. The sounds inside and outside the room. The gaps between the sounds. The space beyond your immediate surroundings. Notice its endlessness. Feel the silence. Feel time's timelessness.

10 / The Lotus Eaters:
Remembering to Practice

Odysseus sets sail for Ithaca. He spends exactly seventeen days at sea, and on the eighteenth day, as he's about to land, Poseidon, his great nemesis, god of earthquakes and great storms at sea, realizes how close Odysseus is to shore and sends a horrendous storm that smashes Odysseus' tiny raft to bits. So near and now so far from land, and at the brink of despair, Odysseus bobs up and down in the cold swells, clinging to a piece of driftwood. Two days pass, the storm abates, the shore again appears as the sea calms. Suddenly a wave rises up out of nowhere and smashes Odysseus into a rock; he holds on for dear life as another huge wave crushes him, tearing his fingers away from the rock, sucking him back out to sea. Finally, floating on the waves, he drifts to a place where a calm river runs into the sea. Completely spent, he can do nothing but pray for a good current to draw him in:

> O hear me lord of the stream:
> how sorely I depend on your mercy!
> derelict as I am by the sea's anger.
> Is he not sacred, even to the gods,
> The wandering man who comes, as I have come,
> In weariness before your knees, your waters?[1]

There are times when there is nothing to do but pray, to ask someone or something, even if we don't know who, for help. This is one of the great messages of *The Odyssey* and one of the great lessons we learn from the disasters we suffer on our journey home: though we must make tremendous efforts, we can't go it alone. The self-help books won't work. Awash in the sea of our own stories, all we can do is supplicate the gods, even though they are unreliable. But our prayers are not futile. As Odysseus here expresses, when we pray we see that exactly because we have made our best effort and spent ourselves in doing so, we have become sacred. He or she is sacred who comes wandering in weariness in these waters, to swim, float, or sink.

I have a Zen friend who has been a monk for thirty years or so. Over all that time he has been faithful to his practice and has, at least to the outward eye, done quite well. But a few years ago he began to talk to me about how frightened he felt inside. He had worked out over the years good ways of coping with his fear so that it didn't bother him much, and it was unnoticeable to others. But he was beginning to find this constant coping no longer acceptable. He came to talk to me. But what could I say? He was already meditating, already doing all the things I usually recommend that people do—and he had been doing those things for years. I couldn't help him. Some time later he came back to talk to me. He told me that he had figured out what to do: he asked for help. "Who do you ask?" I inquired. "I don't know," he told me. "When I feel the fear I just say, 'Please help me,' out loud if no one is around, or silently." "Is it working?" I asked him. "Yes it is." A year or two later he came again to see me. He said he was still working on the practice of asking for help but that now he wanted to extend the practice. He looked me in the eye, with tears streaming down his face. "Please help me," he said to me.

⚬⟋⟍

Is it possible that you too need help? Maybe you already know you do, believe in God, and pray to God for help every day. But how sincere is your prayer? And how much do you really feel your need? Do you pray only because it is your habit and your belief? Take a moment to ask yourself these questions.

Or maybe it has never occurred to you that you could ask for help, because you know that the sort of help you need is not the help any of your friends or family could provide. And you don't know who else to ask.

Close your eyes now and return to yourself. Be your breathing and be the feeling of your body sitting in your chair. From this settled place make a prayer asking for help. Ask God if you want to. Or don't ask God: just ask, as my friend asked without knowing whom he was asking. Maybe this is closer to who God really is anyway: the One Whom we can't know. Whoever you ask, just ask.

Please help me. Please help me.

Breathe the words. Ask as deeply, as sincerely, as you can.

The tide turns and Odysseus is washed ashore, where, naked and exhausted, he crawls under an olive tree to sleep. He has landed on Skeria, land of the Phaiakians, a people expert in the sailing arts and known for their kindness: it is their principle that they will make sure that anyone who is washed ashore on their land receives safe passage home—no matter the difficulty. The king welcomes Odysseus and prepares a sumptuous banquet. After the eating and drinking and the customary athletic contests, there is an evening performance by a lyre-playing bard, whose songs tell of the exploits of heroes. When the bard sings of Odysseus' own exploits, Odysseus weeps secretly, covering himself with a shawl. The weeping is therapeutic; Odysseus requests more songs, songs about Troy, and hearing these, his weeping grows stronger and stronger, until he is like "a woman weeping for her husband who has fallen in battle, who clings to the fallen man's body in her grief, shrieking and wailing as she's dragged away."[2]

As we've already had occasion to note, the past is sad: even the glorious times, remembered long afterward, seem melancholy, for good as they might have been, they are gone. There is nothing we can or need to do about them, and so, unlike the present and the future, which always come with problems and issues to be resolved, the past is complete—which makes it all the sadder. And if the past we are recalling is not pleasant, if it includes the pain of missed opportunities, disappointments or misdeeds, how much more anguished is its recollection. As we grow older, the past becomes a wider and deeper ocean. The sea of stories washes us this way and that, and though, like Odysseus, we may be able to keep the emotional impact of this concealed from others, and perhaps even from ourselves, still its effect on us is powerful.

Noticing how the song has affected Odysseus, the king asks him to reveal his identity and tell his story, and this request begins the five-books-long flashback that tells of his famous exploits.

Here is the story Odysseus tells:

Ten years ago, leaving Troy, Odysseus and his men sacked a city on their way home. Remember, Odysseus is no paragon of virtue. He is an ordinary person like you, with ordinary passions, who does ordinary things. A seafaring warrior, in need of booty and provisions, he naturally sacks a city, as anyone would. But this time he meets resistance, is beaten back, and he flees back into the sea, where he again becomes Poseidon's victim.

Blown far off course, Odysseus and his remaining men wash up finally onto the Land of the Lotus Eaters, a peaceful people who mean no harm and are happy to share with Odysseus' scouting party the honey-sweet lotus fruit on which they live. No sooner do the scouts eat the fruit than they forget themselves and their purpose. They give themselves over so completely to forgetting that they don't go back to the ship to report to Odysseus; they forget their wish to go home, forget there is anything else to do but eat lotus fruit on this lovely island. Odysseus has to find them, drag them forcibly back to the ship, and strap them into their seats beside the mighty oars.

The other day I was talking to a Zen practitioner who told me about a particular meditation practice he was working on. He was contemplating a spiritual phrase throughout his workday, using it as a theme to accompany and contextualize all his activities. The practice, he said, was quite powerful and bracing, and it wasn't hard to do, at least when he actually could do it. The hard part was remembering to do it. In fact, he said, most of the time, absorbed in this or that issue at work, he'd forget about it, and by the end of the week he'd all but lost track of it.

I knew exactly what he was talking about. Spiritual practice is quite easy; it's remembering to do it that's hard. I often ask people to try an experiment: find a room with a doorway on either end. Place in your mind an important spiritual intention or aspiration. Now mindfully walk through the doorway and across the room toward the other doorway and see if you can keep the intention in your mind. Most people report that by the time they reach the doorway at the other end of the room they've forgotten several times. This is what we're up against, this is the normal human everyday mind, fickle and easily distracted. And how much more difficult to remember our spiritual practice, our deepest intentions, motivations, and aspirations, when we are intoxicated with our lives, when, like Odysseus' men, we're feasting on pleasant-tasting lotus roots someone has given us.

This theme of forgetting, of losing track of what's important, of being sidetracked time and again, whether by pleasure or fear or laziness, is one of *The Odyssey*'s great themes. You could argue that, of all the adversities that Odysseus faces on his journey home, the tendency for him or his men to be sidetracked, to forget their purpose, is the most difficult to overcome because it is so slippery. Poseidon's storms are crushing, giants and demons unnerving, but these are, at least, present and clear dangers to be overcome by endurance and main strength. How much more difficult it is to notice when your attention simply wanders, when you forget what you are doing, and to rouse yourself back on course. It's almost as if we depend on the large disasters—the broken relationships, financial setbacks, the illnesses—just to keep us on track. In many ways, Odysseus' most dangerous enemy is his own tendency to be pleasantly and mindlessly sidetracked.

Deep down we are all quite clear about what we truly want and need in this lifetime; even if we can't name it, or find access to it, we know that what we call values or meaning or life's purpose— some path toward truth, love, goodness—is the most important thing in our lives. Yet we lose track of it constantly: we can't even walk across a room without losing track of it. There are good reasons for this, practical reasons. We have to earn a living, take care of the house, the family, keep up our social life, get some exercise, stay informed about world and local events, volunteer, get the car fixed, pick up the clothes at the cleaners. These things take time and focus and they wear us out. But also we're just plain lazy, filling our days and nights with pointless activity, which is so easy to do when we have such a plethora of attractive, seemingly consequential, but actually trivial choices at our disposal.

I think of the Lotus Eaters as the original hippies. Stoned on lotus fruit, they live pleasant lives, full of peace and love. There's nothing terribly objectionable about this. Life's dreamy pleasures have their place. Why not relax and enjoy, not get bent out of shape by our drivenness? But when we have a commitment to the journey home, we have to cast off such distractions—again and again, because they keep on coming back, in different disguises. Maybe they're disguised as a need to accomplish something important, but are actually a cover for our fear of facing ourselves. Maybe they steal up on us as a desire for relief, enjoyment, or enhancement that we feel is our due and our right. Or maybe getting wrapped up in our own stories and the stories of our friends is the lotus fruit we mindlessly munch, without realizing we are doing so.

Spiritual practice can be a lotus fruit, too. The calmness of meditation, the comfort of a sermon, the powerful and intoxicating sense of certainty and inspiration that belief can bring—all these can be pleasant distractions that seem nourishing but can become like side roads leading us away from the truth of our lives and toward a happy, spiritually-tinged fantasy.

How can we know if we're fooling ourselves? How can we tell we've gone off track? What are the sure signs that show us that what we think is the journey's way is actually a seductive dead end? It's hard to say. We just have to pay attention, trust the feedback we get from inside and out, and be willing to have the courage to change course when we've gone off.

Having had the rare experience of living for many years in a semimonastic spiritual community, I know that sometimes the contemplative life can actually be a path of avoidance. More than once, in my capacity as a leader, I had to ask people who felt they were doing fine to leave the community for their own good, because it was clear to me and other leaders that their forward movement along the path had stalled, and they were now marking time. Again, there's nothing objectionable about marking time. We all do that once in a while; it's part of the process. But when there's been more than enough time marking, and when it's clear from a person's aggressive or resistant or erratic behavior that he himself is not comfortable with it, but can't admit this to himself or anyone else, and doesn't know what to do about it, then it's good if someone like Odysseus can come along, drag him by the heels back to the ship, and strap him into his seat. Dealing with such situations was never an easy task, and I was always heartened, whenever, usually years later, people thanked me for the help I had given that didn't seem to them like help at the time.

11 / Being Nobody

I n ancient Greek culture, qualities of trickiness or cleverness were associated with civilization, the ability to craft and
refine nature. This civilized craftiness is part of our internal process as well: simply growing up and managing to survive in this
complicated, contentious world, we all craft stories that are partly
true and partly false, semblances of an identity we can present
to the world as a coherent and, we hope, effective face. Wiliness,
craftiness, and deception are major themes for us, too, and they
come strongly into play in Odysseus' next disaster.

Odysseus and his men land on the Cyclopes' island. Unlike
Odysseus, and unlike us, the Cyclopes possess no craftiness
whatsoever. They live naturally and roughly, without refinement.
They don't build houses, they live in caves. They don't cultivate
fields, but subsist on meat and milk provided by their livestock.
They live apart from one another, without ever meeting in assembly—each one a law unto himself and his family. They don't make
ships, so they can't search out other lands, other points of view.
One-eyed, they have no depth perception. Isolated from the world
and from one another, the Cyclopes occupy themselves with the
rudimentary business of eating, sleeping, and herding. They have
no culture, no skills, no wiles. But being alone, being unrefined,
being self-sufficient has given them one advantage: it has made
them large, very large. In fact they are giants.

Sometimes, weary of all our artifices, we long to be natural, to throw off our stories and just "be ourselves." But this isn't as simple as it sounds. For as much as we may find ourselves beleaguered by our stories, they also protect us, and provide us with something crucial that we need. The Cyclopes are creatures who are just being themselves. They are as we would be without our wiles, crafts, skills, deceptions, and stories. They don't need a social face, for they do not communicate with others. Without communication, without exchange and interrelation, the ego can grow without restraint, becoming rough, crude, unbridled. Natural and unchecked, feeding on the fat of the land, the ego grows huge, self-obsessed, with no concern for others or cognizance of them. This self becomes sloppy, gross, and bold. In this the ego is half blind like a one-eyed Cyclops, seeing only self, but not other. And this lack of perception and parallax, as we will soon see, is a vulnerable condition.

Odysseus and his men, in need of provisions, stumble into the cave of the Cyclops Polyphemos, who at the moment is away tending to his flocks. They feast on cheese and milk and are about to sneak away, but Odysseus, in one of his many disastrous lapses of judgment, will not let them go. He is curious to see what kind of people the Cyclopes are. Hospitality to strangers is a cardinal virtue in ancient Greek culture, as we saw with Odysseus on Skeria, and with Telemachus hosting Athena on Ithaca. In their island culture, a stranger arriving on a ship is welcomed, fed, given gifts—even before his name is asked. So Odysseus decides to remain in the Cyclops' cave, awaiting his return, in expectation of this sort of civilized treatment.

But when Polyphemos returns, he shuts the cave door behind him with a mammoth stone so heavy that it would take twenty-two large chariots, we are told, to move it. Odysseus and his men are terrified by his entrance and cower in a corner, unable to announce themselves. When Polyphemos discovers his intruders (who are as small as mice to him), he laughs heartily and asks them who they are and where they come from. Clever Odysseus is never one to tell the truth in trying circumstances, so, naturally, he lies and says their ship has been destroyed and they have come seeking shelter and hospitality. The Cyclops ignores this request for help. In a scene depicted with gory detail, he dashes the brains of a few of the men against the cave walls, eating them up with gusto—bones, organs, and all—washing it all down with pailfuls of goat's milk. Odysseus and his remaining men are horrified.

Feeling he has nothing to fear from his pathetic tiny guests, Polyphemos goes to sleep. Odysseus sharpens his sword ready to take revenge for his slaughtered crewmen, but he quickly realizes that doing so will seal their own doom—for he and his men would never be able to lift the huge stone that bars the door. Killing Polyphemos will trap them inside the cave forever. The next morning Polyphemos wakes and has a few more men for breakfast. Clearly Odysseus needs a scheme. He prepares a huge stake, sharpened at one end and cured in the fire. When the Cyclops returns from his daily herding, Odysseus offers him a splendid special wine, and Polyphemos drinks to his heart's content, becoming quite drunk. Tell me your name, he asks Odysseus, and I will give you a guest gift. "My name is Nobody," Odysseus answers, and Polyphemos says, "Wonderful, Mr. Nobody, the guest gift I will give you is that you will be the last one I eat." And with this he falls into a drunken stupor.

Now Odysseus and a few of his strongest men plunge the burning stake into Polyphemos' single eye. He bellows with pain and, blinded, rages and calls for help. Other Cyclopes come to the cave door shouting, "What is going on in there? Is someone attacking you in some way?" Polyphemos replies, "Nobody is attacking me! Nobody is killing me now by trickery and deception!" The other Cyclopes say, "Well, then, it must be that the gods have it in for you, so there is nothing we can do." And off they go. The next morning when Polyphemos lets his herds out through the cave door, Odysseus and his men escape, strapped onto the undersides of sheep to avoid detection.

There's no escaping the moral of this tale: when faced with the violence of overblown egotism, being Nobody is the best escape. The craft of being Nobody is the antidote to the dumb brutality of self-centeredness.

In some spiritual circles egolessness or selflessness is a major concern. This has never sounded quite right to me. Even the effort to be "good" sounds too idealistic, too much to deny the pungent quirkiness of our human character and the persistence of our wily stories. Besides, it seems quite doubtful that we would ever actually be able to achieve selflessness, egolessness, or goodness. The continual effort to achieve this unachievable goal would make us even more dissatisfied with our lives than we were before. Wouldn't it be better simply to try to be ourselves, in the faith that doing this with a minimum of confusion will be sufficient? But this also is no small task. Few of us are willing to actually be ourselves. Mostly we deny, berate, or ignore ourselves, preferring self-deception, judgmentalism, or just plain oblivion. Being ourselves involves awareness and acceptance of our craftiness and our imperfection—and this awareness tames us, so that we can understand and appreciate our quirks and the quirks of others. It gives a broader, deeper perspective. Perfection is not our spiritual goal. We do not aspire to be Nobody. We are and need to be Somebody, wily and crafty enough to interact with others, but avoiding the risk of puffing ourselves up and becoming swollen and blind with self-concern. But to be Somebody in a balanced way, without overdoing it as the Cyclopes do, we need to appreciate the experience of being Nobody from time to time.

To be Nobody is not to enter some fantastic condition of egolessness. It is simply to be willing and able, when it is time, to drop the self, to let Somebody go and surrender to circumstances. We do this as a discipline when we give ourselves over in meditation or in prayer. We do it, too, in those rare but always absorbing moments of abandonment that can come in art or work or love. We might need to do it at any moment of living—to let go on a moment's notice of what we think we are and what we think we want, and to be willing to turn around on a dime, trusting what comes instead of evaluating and resisting it. To be Nobody is to float on the ocean of stories with faith, and without thrashing around too much, willing to wait for the proper current to take us where we need to go.

I have a friend who worked as a lawyer in Washington, D.C. His job was high-pressured and fast-paced, in a high-pressured and fast-paced town, which is a crazy world unto itself. It was always my friend's dream to be Somebody, to operate at the highest levels of society, not so he could be important, but so that he could effect the sorts of changes in the world he deeply believed in. For years he functioned quite successfully. He advanced, he made things happen. He also made plenty of money, and gained a good reputation. But there was a great personal and psychic cost. Year by year he could feel his soul and his heart sinking with the stress of the constant effort to be Somebody, with no rejuvenating time or space to be Nobody. Finally, after ten or so years of this life, he suffered a complete mental and emotional collapse. He had no choice but to take time off from his firm for healing, and to reassess his situation.

He came home to California and we got together a few times. I could feel him slowly turning his life over in his mind, ruminating about what had happened, and where to go from here. The choice, he finally felt, came down to this: whether to understand his breakdown as an aberration, an abnormality, due to overwork, and so to patch himself up with rest and medications and reenter the fray. Or, on the other hand, to see the breakdown not as a malady, but as the ordinary response of an ordinary person to a very trying situation, and to admit that, like anyone, he was human and therefore vulnerable. My friend opted for the second view. He saw that he could not simply get over his troubles as quickly as possible and go on being Somebody as if they'd never happened. He needed to integrate his breakdown into his life and personality, and resume his career on a new basis. My friend took quite a while to heal, but eventually he did return to legal practice, although not in Washington, and with a new vision of himself not as the mover and shaker he'd imagined himself to be, but as a person whose mission was to help individuals in whatever way he could through his legal work. To become a sustainable Somebody he first had to accept that he was, like all of us, Nobody.

In ancient Greek culture, as in our own, so much hinges on protecting a good name. Indeed, without concern for name and position very little would happen in this world. It's not a bad thing to have pride in one's accomplishments and reputation. If the Achaeans had not been concerned for their honor and for the glory of victory, they would not have marched off to Troy for war; and with no going out, there would have been no coming home. We all need a name, a place, an identity. But we also need to be willing to enter our condition as Nobody, as a foundation for whatever else we may be.

If no longer a mother, what else?

Sometimes we enter this condition quite suddenly and unexpectedly. Another friend, who is extremely bright, accomplished, and perceptive, is only in his forties, but has already mastered several professions: trained as a physician, he later became a scholar of medical history, and some years after that went to law school and now is a practicing attorney specializing in medical cases. In personal matters he is scrupulous to a fault, and seems always to understand not only what a person is saying, but also what the person really means, beyond what is said. He has helped me with many things over the years that I have been unable to figure out how to handle on my own. A broken water main, a legal hassle, a financial issue—of all these things he is master. But, he tells me, it is exhausting being him! His mind is so active, his spirit so searching, that there seems to be no rest at all. Aware of so many possibilities in this world—of the many opportunities for gain and growth, of the even greater number of chances for disaster—he is constantly thinking and scheming in one direction or another. He has done many Zen retreats, which give him a great deal of peace and relief (he is also a skilled meditator with an uncommon ability to focus his mind on a meditation object and let it quiet) but as soon as they are over he is back to the burden of being himself.

One day he had an astonishing experience at a business meeting of his law firm. Someone was talking and my friend suddenly and for no particular reason became completely absorbed in listening to what the person was saying—merely listening, without evaluation, without considering options for advantage or pitfalls of disadvantage, but simply listening, totally, utterly listening. "I was listening so completely I disappeared," he told me. The experience was completely absorbing. But suddenly he came back to himself. It was like waking up from a dream. He realized in that moment that he had lost control, that he wasn't himself. And then he became quite terrified. The whole experience lasted only a moment or two and then he was fine. In the weeks afterward, digesting the experience, he came to feel that it was soothing and relieving to lose himself that completely. Though he had become frightened a moment afterward, in the moment of disappearance he felt more peace than he had ever known before.

Emily Dickinson wrote of this being Nobody with a healthy dose of humor:

> *I'm Nobody! Who are you?*
> *Are you — Nobody — Too?*
> *Then there's a pair of us?*
> *Don't tell! They'd advertise — you know!*
>
> *How dreary — to be — Somebody!*
> *How public — like a Frog —*
> *To tell one's name—the livelong June—*
> *To an admiring Bog!*[1]

The Polyphemos story doesn't end with Odysseus' bloody and daring escape from the cave. There's an important coda. As he sails away, Odysseus can't resist crowing about his cleverness. He shouts out to Polyphemos that he got what he deserved, and that if he wants to know who's responsible, it was he, Odysseus, son of Laertes, from Ithaca, who is to blame. Polyphemos, sightless but hearing Odysseus' voice, goes into a fury, scoops up a nearby mountain, and hurls it in the direction of the ship. It misses, but the impact causes a swell that pulls the fleet all the way back to the island. Odysseus manages to escape again, but not before Polyphemos curses his name, praying to Poseidon, his father, to prevent Odysseus' safe return, but that if it can't be prevented that Odysseus "come late, in bad case, with loss of all his companions, in someone else's ship, and find troubles in his household."[2] This curse is the cause of all Odysseus' further troubles. It explains why Poseidon plagues him for ten years, why every time he's set sail he becomes storm-tossed. Polyphemos' cursing wish foretells exactly what will befall Odysseus on his journey home.

So it seems that Odysseus' troubles have been of his own making. It seems that although in a pinch he is clever enough to be Nobody, his pride is still strong, compelling him to push things to a bad end.

This seems quite true to life. Accepting that we are Nobody isn't easy. It might come at great personal cost to us, and even if we happen on it quite by chance, it can be frightening at first. But digesting the experience of being Nobody doesn't cure us forever from the pride and egotism that can bring down curses on us just when we think escape is at hand. It's said in many Buddhist texts that only the highest spiritual adepts can see through the subtle pride of self-clinging. Even the ability to enter deep meditation states and experience strong wisdom insights does not ensure that you won't be tripped up from time to time by your long habit of needing to be Somebody that others admire and envy. I have seen such tripping up happen on a regular basis in myself, in experienced spiritual practitioners, and sometimes too, more spectacularly, in colleagues, spiritual teachers who have created enormous troubles for themselves and their communities through the weirdness that can come with that little unacknowledged piece of destructive egotism, all too often masked by exceptional spiritual power. What towering waves and flashing lightning bolts have I seen it hurl down!

Interestingly, Odysseus' mistake here is also, in a way, not a mistake. Though it leads to many further disasters and troubles, these are just the disasters and troubles he needs to bring him home at the right time and in the right way.

12 / Fatigue

Living with our double nature, as Nobody and Somebody, can be exhausting sometimes. Our minds, addicted to clarity, sometimes wear down with the effort to relax into the enigmatic flow of our murky lives. We become confused about what we're after, who we are, what we're doing. We know we want to return home to the person we were meant to be, to the life we know is really ours, but as soon as we come close to it we lose confidence; we are turned around by the world's compelling images and something tempting or distracting causes us to lurch in the other direction. Paradox, ambivalence, and conflicting desires beset us, and even though we make a valiant effort to sort it all out, we can't help ourselves: worn out from the inner battle, we fall asleep at just the wrong time, sometimes even within sight of shore . . .

Leaving the Cyclopes, Odysseus sails to the pleasant Aeolian shore, where King Aeolus hosts him sumptuously for a month and then sends him on with a most useful guest gift—a bagful of ill winds. What good is this? If the winds are kept in the bag they won't plague Odysseus' ships, and he will have smooth sailing home to Ithaca. And this is precisely what happens. For nine blissful days Odysseus and his men sail effortlessly on. Mindful that this is to be the last leg of the journey (or so he believes!), and aware of all the trouble he's been through, Odysseus is taking no chances. He personally sees to the care of the ships in full detail, all day and all night long, day after day, working himself so hard that when they are nearly at the Ithacan shore ("so close we could see men tending fires on the beaches"), he is overcome with an insurmountable fatigue. And now, just as the journey's almost done, and so relieved by the sight of home he can't help himself, Odysseus falls fast asleep.

As he snoozes, the men begin talking among themselves. It's unfair that Odysseus gets all the credit and all the bounty, they say. After all, they've been sharing the journey with Odysseus step by step, and many of them (in fact, by the time we're finished, all of them) have perished. And when gifts are handed out—like that gold or silver they imagine to be in the sack that Odysseus has been hoarding secretly from them throughout the voyage out from Aeolus—they always go to Odysseus, never to them. The crew's resentment and complaining builds. With Odysseus asleep there's no one to temper them and finally the men are emboldened to open the sack: if these treasures are not for them at least they can see, while the boss sleeps, what they look like. As soon as the sack is opened the ill winds rush out, and the enormous storms that result blow the ship back out to sea, on and on, nine days backward, all the way back to Aeolus—just as in the last disastrous episode the ships were blown back to the Cyclopes' island. How many times, we too might ask ourselves, do we have to be blown back to start over again before we attain our goal and touch the shores of home?

When Odysseus wakes up and realizes what has happened he is so disheartened that he wants to leap overboard. But he doesn't. He holds on in the heavy squalls and hides his face so his crew will not see the despair he feels. When they return bedraggled to King Aeolus to tell their tale and ask for further help, the king refuses. Since the gods appear to be so much against you, he tells them, I will have nothing more to do with you.

How close we can come to home. We can be nearly there. Maybe we *are* there. But at the last minute the pressure of our arrival is so great we can't stand it. We have so much wanted to come home, have worked so long for it, have been through so many disasters and troubles along the way that we've gotten used to looking ahead, used to our longing. It's become so ingrained, so familiar, that it's almost comfortable, almost an identity. So when the shores of home are within reach we panic. We find we are afraid of what we most desire. The fires on the beach, so warm and familiar, are at the same time terrifying. Who will we be if we land here? Our unacknowledged ambivalence (and we've been pulling and hauling as hard as we can to keep it unacknowledged) wears us out. We fall asleep almost on purpose. And while we sleep unruly forces within us stir up our self-destructive impulses. We open up the bag of our self-restraint and our dark passions come streaming out, blowing us all over the place. We were so close and now we are as far away as we have ever been. No wonder the experience leaves us dazed, exhausted, and confused. No wonder we fall into despair.

This is a story that perhaps you can recognize. I could tell stories of friends I have known who've been through it, but you have your own stories. They go like this: a person spends years building a life, going through the struggle of establishing a career, a family, possibly a degree of prominence, wealth, or accomplishment— and just when he can finally relax and enjoy it all, he decides, quite unconsciously, to blow up his life, to screw things up spectacularly just when fruition seems close at hand. Sometimes this happens through a sexual indiscretion (why, one wonders, would someone create such big trouble for such small pleasure?), through a crazy business or professional decision (how, one wonders, after so many astute moves, could someone make such an obviously stupid move?), or through addiction or some other health disaster seemingly brought on on purpose. But we need not wonder at this. When the fatigue caused by inner spiritual conflict grows deep enough, we fall asleep. And when we're asleep the inner or outer crew conspires, and out of their jealousy and perversion open up the bag of our irrational passions to let fly some destructive wind to blow us back a million miles.

Sometimes the story is less dramatic. Maybe it's the story of one who, without fanfare, simply works against herself in small ways day by day. She has become so used to longing for a future that will never come, so insistent on being the unfulfilled person she thinks she is, that she secretly resists all the things in her life she thinks she's working toward. So she lives at cross-purposes with herself, working hard to achieve what she fears and doesn't really want to achieve, as if actually achieving it would swallow her up. The effort it takes to live this way, running as fast as she can in two opposing directions at once, is exhausting. Overcome with fatigue, she falls asleep, and while she sleeps her life's passions engulf her. She becomes depressed or comes down with an illness. Or maybe there is no illness or depression that anyone can recognize or name. Just the slow spiritual erosion of discouragement and disillusionment that is quite unnoticeable to others as she continues to go through the motions of living.

So Odysseus, groaning heavily, and full of grieving, leaves Aeolus' palace, takes to his ships, and sails on, though his men's spirits were "worn away with the pain of rowing and [their] own silliness, since homecoming seemed [theirs] no longer."[1]

13 / Circe, or Desire

After a disastrous interlude in the Laestrygonian land, where swarms of the gigantic inhabitants spear his men like fish, and destroy all but one of his ships, Odysseus lands exhausted on the Aenian island, as low as he has ever been. The few men left are traumatized by all that's happened. When they see a curl of smoke rising up from the land, they quake in their boots with fear: what horrific personage awaits them now? When Odysseus suggests they investigate, the men burst into tears, and fall down weeping and wailing. Finally he convinces them that they have no choice. They will die without help. So the remaining crew is divided into two platoons, one to guard the ship, the other to investigate the island. They cast lots. It falls to Eurylochus' band to go forth to explore the island.

They come to a house surrounded by wolves, lions, jackals, and other beasts: horrible creatures that paw at the men but do not attack. Inside, the sorceress goddess Circe sits at her magnificent loom weaving a luminous shawl of shimmering glory as she sings enchanting songs that put the men at their ease, drawing them toward her. They enter and she offers them refreshment, which is, however, laced with a potion that, "wipe[s] from their memories any thought of home."[1] Instantly they are changed into swine. Only Eurylochus, who'd sensed a trap, manages to escape. He runs back to the ship to report what he has seen, but is so horrified by the experience that he's rendered literally speechless, and it takes him a long while to recover and finally speak.

The story so far tells us several things. First, that our commitment to return home is wobbly and vulnerable—we are easily seduced, turned into swine, docile beasts easily manipulated by a goddess, or a government, a group, an ideology, or our own basest and most destructive impulses. Second, we learn again, and more deeply, as Telemachus showed us when he was finally able to free himself from stasis by speaking his grief into the assembly, that life can traumatize us, sometimes even without our knowing it, rendering us speechless for a while, and that only when we finally speak the truth can the action of our story advance.

As it does here: Eurylochus finds his tongue. He pleads that they cut their losses and flee the island immediately but Odysseus insists that that would be impossible. He must see to this problem and rescue the men. "Necessity drives me on," he says.[2] This is noteworthy. Odysseus is capable of retreat, and often does flee in the face of difficult challenges. He knows there are times when it is better to go backward than forward, but there are other times when, though the chances of disaster are very great, he is moved to press on. And this is such a time.

On the way to meet Circe, the god Hermes appears and gives Odysseus instructions, and, not incidentally, a counterpotion. The instructions are these: First, take the counterpotion. When Circe offers you her potion, take it, it will not affect you. Then draw your sword and threaten to run her through. She will be frightened and will offer to sleep with you. Sleep with her. But only after she has released your men from their pig bodies and sworn never again to cause you harm.

Odysseus does all this. Released, the men appear younger, stronger, and more beautiful than they were before they became pigs. When they see Odysseus they burst into tears again and weep and wail for some time. Odysseus returns to the ship and tells the others what has happened, urging them all to join together in Circe's palace: Circe won't hurt us now, he assures them, for a goddess's word is good as gold. But Eurylochus is terrified to go. It's a trap, it won't work, he says. He speaks passionately and mutinously of Odysseus' many mistakes—how his foolhardiness and pride had put them at risk so many times. If he, Odysseus, had left Polyphemos' cave when the others had wanted to, that bloody disaster would never have taken place. If he had not taunted the Cyclops, there would have been no curse, and Poseidon would not have become their enemy. If he had not fallen asleep at the wrong time the disaster of the Aeolian winds would not have happened. If, if, if, if. Blame, blame, blame, blame.

We are like Eurylochus, full of blame and regret. It can be perfectly true: we or someone else is to blame; things could or should be better. But this line of thought and emotion is fairly useless. We need to cut through it, cut out the bellyaching. Odysseus is aware of this and does not fall prey to the paralysis of guilt or regret. He meets the outburst resolutely, drawing his sword, ready to run Eurylochus through on the spot, but his men restrain him. Overriding Eurylochus' complaints, Odysseus convinces the men that the only way is forward, to Circe's palace. When they are reunited there with their fellows (those who were formerly pigs), there are more tears, a riot of emotion. The brave ancient Greek warriors are surprisingly and spectacularly emotional.

And there they remain, feasting for a year! A full year of drinking and eating and lounging around in Circe's palace. And presumably, for Odysseus, nights of love with the alluring goddess. Odysseus seems to have forgotten his purpose again. Things seem to be going so pleasantly. But this time his men bring him back to his senses, and urge him to press on with the journey. He remembers what he needs to do. Circe agrees to help them move on to the next destination.

What does this story tell us? That what's alluring, what's dangerous, the shimmering enchanting thing that perhaps we ought to flee from because it might turn us into beasts, cannot be avoided.

You cannot run away from your desires, despite your terror and the mutiny that is brewing within your heart. If it turns out that you are transformed into a pig, well, you can be turned back into a person again, and you'll be better off having seen life from the other side. So yes, you must embrace what's enchanting, shimmering, alluring, and dangerous within you sometimes—but not naïvely, not without some fortification, some counterpotion, some instructions for how to proceed. Your spiritual practice, the meditation, prayers, or reflection that you do with a spirit of discipline and repetition, gives you not only courage, but also some necessary skill. You can go into the fire—but with the proper protection. And then you'll be all right. The relief you'll feel when you've gotten through this most difficult of passages will be so great that after you stop weeping with gratitude you'll want to enjoy yourself for a while. Maybe you'll feast on your brilliant escape for a whole year, simply basking in the glow of your accomplishment, feeling as if there's no need to go on any further. But eventually you'll recognize that you're not home yet. There is still a long way to go.

The Circe story reminds me of a very poignant event that once happened to a close friend of mine. Happily married for many years, he suddenly found himself in a compelling flirtation with a much younger woman. She was just as passionately involved with him as he was with her. The feelings that were aroused in both of them were powerful. They both felt awake, aroused, open to life and love in ways they had never experienced before. On one hand the man was fascinated with these feelings, inexorably drawn forward into them. On the other, he loved and respected his wife; he had no desire to hurt her or to diminish their relationship in any way. Clear that he could not start an illicit love affair, he thought that the only thing he could do was to break off the confusing if wonderful relationship. The young woman reluctantly agreed, for she also respected the man's wife and had no desire to cause harm. Yet the man's heart told him that it was not right to stop seeing the young woman, that there was something important in their coming together. What to do? When I heard about the situation from my friend I was at first afraid for him and his wife. But then I thought, "After all, how can love be a bad thing? Maybe there's a way to appreciate what's going on without anyone being too hurt by it." All three were good people, wishing the best for one another. They were courageous as well, capable of holding the difficulty of the situation within the arms of the spiritual practice they had all been committed to for a long time. It was very confusing, but they were willing to talk to one another honestly about what was going on. All three of them, at different times, bounced back and forth between elation and despair. The man and the young woman did continue their friendship, with his wife's consent, and without any sexuality between them. The two friends' being together evolved and deepened, enriching them both, and awakening something necessary in each of them. Something was also awakened in the man's wife and within their relationship. They began to see a need to rediscover each other. So in the end love *did* turn out to be a good thing, and going forward with it, tricky as it was, was powerfully beneficial for everyone involved.

We all have tremendous passions and desires that scare us. Our unconscious wants and needs are illicit, immense, and immensely impractical and dangerous. Whether it is for sexual escapades or for power, luxury, or knowledge, we all have insatiable thirsts that we know would do us in if we ever tried to slake them. And certainly our lusts are dangerous. Most of us choose wisely to ignore them. But if we want to journey home to who we really are, we have to find a way to go forward into even our most alluring desires, without being turned permanently into pigs.

A clue to how we might be able to manage this rather delicate and risky operation can be seen in the way the warriors deal with the extravagant display of emotion in this episode. In our modern culture, bravery and determination are associated with emotional repression. Contemporary superheroes are men of steel who disappear completely into their goals. They are nothing but their efforts to defeat the enemy, capture the criminal, prevent the disaster. While these goals may be noble, the point is not how noble the heroes are but how tough and ruthless. They will stop at nothing to get the job done. And after it is done they do not rejoice or celebrate, they simply press on to the next challenge. It's true that in some contemporary stories heroes are understood to have some tragic past that drives them on, but we never see any expression of their emotion, and the point seems to be that nonexpression of emotion gives us strength and energy for doing what we need to do.

There is something startling, then, about these ancient Greek warriors who scream, cry, or quake in their boots with terror, despair, or gratitude. Possibly we can learn from them that we can survive the full expression of emotions, even seemingly contradictory emotions. This expression is even necessary, and not incompatible with our deepest, most important goals. The energy we think we are preserving in holding back from our emotions may be counterproductive. This is what Odysseus and his men are showing us when they fall into despair, weep, cry out, party, or tremble with fear.

In the Buddhist teachings on working with emotion, honesty about emotions is the most important thing. They acknowledge that unbridled action that comes of anger or hatred or lust is harmful, but at the same time fearlessly appreciate the recognition and expression of emotion, whatever it may be. With meditation and other forms of contemplative practice comes an inner spaciousness large and fluid enough to contain a tremendous range of emotions, and to allow for a full, inner expression of these emotions so that they are appreciated without becoming too dangerous. We bottle up our emotions because we're afraid of what they will do to us—or to others. But having an effective inner life enables us to meet our emotions fully, to trust them and make use of them for our journey outward. Strong emotions that we've long feared can become allies, as we tame and incorporate them into our lives, just as Circe changes from a dangerous sorceress to an important ally for Odysseus and just as my three friends transmuted sexual passion into healing love. Beyond repression of emotions and acting out, this third choice requires some cultivation over time, but can be available to any one of us, if we are courageous and disciplined enough to undertake it. (More about this later.)

One final detail: when Circe sees that her potion has no effect on Odysseus she knows immediately who he is, for a god had prophesied that one day a person would appear who would not be affected by her magic, and that this person would be Odysseus. The same thing had occurred in the Polyphemos story—when Odysseus shouts out his real name Polyphemos remembers that it had been predicted that a man named Odysseus would come one day and put out his eye. Fate and prediction—that which is happening now has been preordained—are featured in almost all mythical and religious literature. It is an imaginative way of saying that our lives are always operating within the sphere of the déjà vu moment, that what is happening now has happened before, will happen again, that our lives are fated, shot through with a palpable sense of destiny. When we act with full attention and full commitment we feel this. I'm not talking about literal predestination or determinism. I'm talking about a feeling we have in our living, when our living is true, of being just right with our lives, exactly aligned with them, as if the life we are living right now is the life we are meant to live, and have always been meant to live. Looking at our life's disasters with this feeling, we see them differently. We see their inevitability and importance. We no longer feel compelled to avoid disaster, to flee or deny. Instead we have a feeling of resoluteness, an interest to go forward into what's difficult, rather than around. We feel "necessity drives us on."

Imagine the shape or flavor of your life's journey so far. Don't think of it as "my life," see it as a story, a tale. Imagine it as an object, a tangible thing. Maybe it is a book like this one that you are holding in your hands. Or a flickering

image you see in front of you. Sit for a moment, with dis-
passion, contemplating this imaginative object. See that it
has a shape, a form, a weight, a presence of its own. See
its integrity, its inevitability. See how snugly its pieces fit
together; if even a single one were moved, the whole shape
would be thrown off. Everything is exactly where it needs
to be.

Now let your mind wander freely. How do you feel about
this object you have been contemplating? What are the
emotions that arise in response to it? Are you able to feel
them fully? Do you flinch, do you hide? Are there emotions
you don't want to experience? Are you willing to experience them anyway?

The life I was meant to live + have lived.

Denial as self protection when young
Denial as wish fulfillment when choosing
    husbands
Forced to face reality — but too late
Punished by suicide of husband
Frightened, guilty, unable to heal
    w/ any other love
Alone so long, relationship no longer
    possible
Exploring deeply solitude as the
    only way to heal + grow

14 / The Land of the Dead

The celebration, as always, must come to an end, and the journey home must continue. Circe tells Odysseus that he must now go to the Land of the Dead, most frightening of all places, to seek a prophecy from Tiresias the blind seer. When he learns that this, not Ithaca, is his next destination, Odysseus falls on his bed and cries. ("I'd no desire / to go on living," he says, "and see the rising light of day.")[1] Once he finishes with the requisite weeping (we all cry at first when disaster strikes; it seems to be what we need to do), he rises up to receive his instructions from Circe.

The Land of the Dead is many things. It is, first of all, the place of our deepest, most unspeakable fears. With the Lotus Eaters we faced a subtle, dangerous enemy, our own forgetfulness. To escape the Cyclops Polyphemos, we had to master the craft of being Nobody. The disaster of the Aeolian winds showed us the pain of our deep spiritual ambivalence. And on Circe's island, we found we needed to include our illicit desires and shameful feelings as allies for the journey home. All these episodes were hair-raising enough, requiring courage and inner resources we didn't know we had. (And we've been through enough by now to know that we're not finished with any of these issues, that they'll all come back one way or another.) But the Land of the Dead is the toughest thing we have seen so far. For here we face the unknown, uncompromising, unappeasable, unnameable force that is out of this world—the force of Death, the Unbeing that wipes away all that's known and all that is. What could be more brutal, more terrifying, than this?

The Land of the Dead is also, as we will see, the land of sacrifice, grief, and forgiveness, for it is the land of the buried past, where we reencounter people now long gone, who had formed our lives, and make a deeper peace with them. We may have thought we'd already done this work. But encountering them now in the Land of the Dead, we integrate their lessons into our lives more deeply. They become who we are and we become them. Though we did not expect it and certainly do not relish it now, it's clear that a visit to the Land of the Dead is necessary. It's a stop we could not have made before. But now that we've experienced the requisite disasters, been humbled and worn out by life's realities and our own repetitive shortcomings, we are ready. I have known many people—at all ages—who have been touched by death, and this has certainly affected them, conditioning their whole lives. But the Odyssean journey to the Land of the Dead comes later in life, after we've traveled long enough to be able to incorporate the lessons we will learn here in a more sober, less romantic way.

Odysseus and his men sail forth "till the sun dipped and all the ways grew dark upon the fathomless unresting sea." They enter a realm of darkness, a place where the sun cannot shine, and beach their ships. Odysseus follows the instructions given him by Circe: he digs a pit and pours libations around it—milk, honey, water, wine, and barley. Then he sacrifices sheep, pouring their blood into the pit, too, to draw the shades to drink. Odysseus is to stand guard at the pit with his sword and chase away all who come, until finally Tiresias appears. After receiving Tiresias' prophecy, Odysseus will entertain visits from other shades, so that he may hear from them truths that are clearer and more final than those of the living. This scene was the inspiration for Dante's *Divine Comedy*, a full three books devoted to a similar truth-confronting visit to the

Land of the Dead, with full Christian elaboration. It may also be the image that drew Sigmund Freud to discover the talking cure: dig a pit, pour libations, make a sacrifice, and then, in the nether world of dreams and automatic thinking, summon the dead (the past and its terrible mythic power) to speak to you truthfully. For lack of knowing such truths we fall ill.

The furious shades circle the pit, mad with thirst, and, though he is "green with fear," Odysseus holds them at bay with his sword. Tiresias finally comes to provide his prophecy, the burden of which is this: Odysseus will make it home but only after much suffering; he will lose all his men and ships, will arrive on Ithaca alone and exhausted, and once there will face further challenges in defeating the suitors; but if he remains patient and steady, keeping his mind's wildness in check, and communicating this forbearance to those around him, whose help he will need, he will in the end be victorious, bringing peace to his household. And above all, Tiresias tells him, you must always be faithful to your journey.

Following Tiresias comes a long parade of visitors who tell their tales, beginning with Anticlea, Odysseus' mother. She is relieved to see her son alive, but worried to find him in this horrible place where mortals never come. She tells Odysseus that she died of grief, fearing for his life when he fought at Troy. This of course saddens Odysseus. Stricken with grief and guilt himself now, he wants to embrace and console her but he can't, for she's only a shade, capable of truth but incapable of offering or receiving physical comfort.

My own mother died long ago, I hope not of grief over me, but I'm not sure. Once, soon after she died, I had a feeling I was speaking to her quite directly through the words of a poem I was writing. It was an uncanny, moving moment that took place late on a full-moon night at Tassajara Zen Mountain Monastery deep in the forested mountains of central California. The words of the poem, her words, came with mesmerizing force, and I felt Odysseus' grief; I heard her truthful words and felt close to her with a sympathy I had not known while she was alive. But much as I wanted to touch and comfort her—and for her to touch and comfort me—to assuage my guilt and grief, I could not embrace her, for she was no longer among the embodied. Years later I heard the poet David Whyte tell of a vivid dream he had of his mother just after her death. She appeared to him as a young woman, at a ball full of people who had populated David's early life, and she spoke words to him that also became part of a poem.

From my own reflections over the years, and from the many intimate stories I have heard about people's spiritual journeys, I have come to appreciate the obvious but too often overlooked importance of the connection we have with our parents. The psychological aspects of this connection have been much studied, but the spiritual dimension is far less mentioned or understood (the biblical injunction to "honor thy father and mother" is more than a moral or a social necessity). The stories of our lives are waves in the mythic ocean; our parents are more than important people to us; our intimate experience of "father" and "mother" includes but goes far beyond the words and deeds of the actual flesh-and-blood human beings who occupy these roles in our lives. Something unspeakably deep and particular is triggered in us with these relationships, and appreciating and healing them (for they always require healing) is an indelible part of our journey home, as Odysseus' encounter with Anticlea here in the Land of the Dead tells us. When we meet our mothers (or our fathers) in the Land of the Dead, our connection to them is clearer and more poignant than it was in life, even though it is incomplete. We need such meetings to sustain us for our ongoing journey. They may take place, as they did in my case, after a parent has passed away, or, if we are lucky, they may take place among the living, as we help our parents through the final days of life and into the passage to death. I suspect they may also take place when we ourselves are close to death, when, in our final moments of reverie, perhaps, our parents appear to us more vividly than they ever had before.

But there's something even more basic going on in this meeting between Odysseus and Anticlea. Our fathers and mothers first introduced us to the other, someone outside ourselves whom we must learn to love, and this is not easy. In fact, in many ways it is impossible. In meeting Anticlea, Odysseus is meeting not only the shade of his mother, but the shade of all the erotic relationships of his life, whose deep structure was formed by his relationship to her. Just as we meet in a particularly intimate way around a campfire, which warms and illuminates our conversation, so here, around the sacrificial pit of blood, Odysseus meets through his mother's shade all those he's loved, to whom he's given himself, from whom he's removed himself, all those he has exalted, failed, honored, and betrayed. He can't embrace them, but in meeting them now, and grieving over what has happened, he finds a measure of healing.

Next follows a parade of many well-known Greek women and men who tell Odysseus their true stories. With each tale the darkness of Death brings the past alive in a new, more mythic way; face-to-face with each one, Odysseus can feel for them, and find a natural forgiveness that doesn't require him either to gloss over or to glorify the past, but only to appreciate it for what it is. In the Land of the Dead there's no more contention. No issues cry out for resolution. Each encounter settles Odysseus, and with each tale his terror diminishes.

Among the visitors is Achilles, champion of the Trojan War, who died gloriously in that immense battle. In life he was truly and fully a hero, powerful, brave, and proud (unlike Odysseus, who, as we've said from the beginning, was always more a man of words and wiles than sword and spear). But Death has taught Achilles something. When Odysseus congratulates him on his glorious demise, and tells him that surely he must be pleased to have garnered such fame for his bravery that he now rules over the Land of the Dead, his name honored and revered, Achilles says, "Let me hear no smooth talk of death from you, Odysseus. Better I say to break sod as a farm hand for some poor country man, on iron rations, than to lord it over all the exhausted dead."[2]

Although we take it for granted that the living desire life and do not want to die, this is not entirely true. Sometimes life gets too involved—there is, after all, always more and more of it, more complication, more trouble, more responsibility. Sometimes in the midst of all this we long for some peace, and we think of death as a prolonged comfortable sleep. As we've seen, Odysseus often falls into despair and longs for the permanent release he imagines he will find in death. But thinking of death as a comfort, as an escape, is wrong. It's a way of avoiding the fact that we simply don't know what death is, and that that's what it is: the unknowable, the incomprehensible, the beyond-all-reach. This is why it is so terrifying. In congratulating Achilles on his noble death, Odysseus imagines that Achilles has found perfect honor and perfect peace now that his life is done. But Achilles' message is clear—death is no picnic. It is backbreaking and exhausting work. It is not the solution to life's difficulties. The realm of life, not the realm of death, is where our journey takes place. Abandoning our pretty fantasies about death and facing our fear of death's inconceivable strangeness is a necessity: for life. Odysseus has to come to the Land of the Dead to hear this once and for all. We do, too.

Death does not provide us with closure. Odysseus meets Ajax the Greater, another brave warrior who committed suicide in shame after a dispute with Odysseus during the battle of Troy. Odysseus feels terrible when he encounters Ajax in the Land of the Dead, and seeks his forgiveness, explaining that he didn't intend any harm. But Ajax says nothing, simply lumbers off, expressionless, and Odysseus does not know whether or not he has been forgiven—or even whether he needs to be.

Many people who have relatives or friends who are close to death are hoping for a peaceful death for the friend and relative, and for themselves some emotional satisfaction in the encounters they imagine might take place in the last weeks or days of life. They're looking for that one conversation, that one look or gesture that will somehow bring to a fruitful and fitting conclusion a lifetime of misunderstanding—or of love. Sometimes those conversations, those gestures or looks do occur. But more often they don't.

And even when they do, it's still no good to put too much spin on them, to be too smug about what they mean or how they will affect us. The shades in the Land of the Dead do not live in a world of peace or closure. Like us they continue to struggle and change. The past, though dead, is not static or finished. It advances and alters as our lives go on. What we do now, how we live now, has a tremendous impact throughout all of time, and beyond. This makes no rational sense, I realize. And in a way it is terrifying. But this is what we see in the Land of the Dead.

As if to underscore the point that death is not a place of peaceful conclusions, Odysseus meets Tantalos and Sisyphus. Tantalos is perpetually burning with thirst as he stands up to his neck in a cool pond his lips can't reach, and is ravenously hungry under boughs full of fruit he can't grab. (His predicament is the source of the English verb *tantalize*.) Sisyphus is pushing his stone endlessly up a hill, and nearly reaching the top when, time after time, the stone rolls down again. These mythical figures recall the various diabolically frustrating situations described in the Buddhist hells. In one Buddhist hell, called the Razor Blade, a man overcome with sexual desire climbs a tree with slashing leaves of razor blades to get to the beautiful woman at the top; when he arrives there the woman disappears, reappearing at the bottom. The razor blades reverse direction as the man climbs back down, and up and down endlessly, lacerating himself with every trip. Then there are the ravenously hungry ghosts, with huge bellies but needle-like throats. There are many more such hellish situations one could cite (Dante is full of them too) all bearing the same clear burden: that our human desire and expectation can never be fulfilled, that even death won't solve it, and that not knowing this and insisting on fulfillment, if not in this world then in the next, make both life and death forms of hell. No, death solves nothing for us. But a visit to the Land of the Dead, if we can stand it, will help us to confront our terror and digest it, so that we will neither avoid death nor fantasize about it, but rather see it for what it is: the mystery of every moment.

There's a Zen story about the Land of the Dead. A master went with his disciple to a funeral. The disciple, deeply concerned with the spiritual matter of "life and death," rapped on the coffin and shouted, "Alive or Dead?" He was asking the master, who replied, "I won't say, I won't say." "Why won't you say?" the desperate disciple asked. "I won't say," the master repeated. On the way home, with the unanswered question of life and death reverberating in his mind, the disciple became more and more agitated. Upset to the point of violence, he turned to the master and said, "If you don't say, I will throttle you." "Go ahead and throttle me," the master said. "I won't say." The disciple did throttle him, and was as a consequence tossed out of the monastery. Years later, the master died, and the disciple came back to the monastery, told the story to the new master, and concluded with the same question as before: "Alive or dead?" "I won't say," the new master replied, at which the disciple was enlightened.

Another Zen disciple asked his teacher, "How is it when one who has died the great death returns to life?" The teacher replied, "He must not go by night: he must get there by daylight." We think that life and death are completely different conditions, that there's an iron curtain separating them, and that once through the curtain there's no coming back. And we think that death is on the dark and scary side of the curtain, life on the bright and merry side. But what do we know? Is it really possible to answer the question "alive or dead?" in a sensible way? Is "the great death" the teacher refers to the same as the "death" we conventionally speak of? Is death Nirvana? Are there heavens and hells? Or is death blankness, nothingness? What could these words possibly designate, other than the hopelessness of language to describe anything beyond itself?

We don't know what death is, nor do we understand life. And without appreciating death we can't appreciate life, and vice versa, because the truth is that we can't say what is life and what is death and what separates the two from each other. There can't be any life without death—each moment we die to that moment; if not, the next moment couldn't come. If the child doesn't die the adult can't appear. So we can't say there is life over here where we are, and death over there in that coffin. Neither can we say that death is a rest, a conclusion, a relief, a closing of the book. A human life ends. That we can say, possibly. But what is death? We can't say. And yet that unsayable fact—that fact of absence or unbeing—is what makes time flow and life go on. To feel this in your bones (because it is not a matter of thinking or understanding something) is to visit the Land of the Dead. It changes you forever.

I have a friend who works as a coach for business executives. Articulate, insightful, and personable, he's quite good at what he does, has been at it for a long time, and is very much in demand in Silicon Valley. When he was a year old, he lost a sister who was just nine months older than he, in the most horrible way: the little girl's clothing caught on fire and she burned to death. Although my friend had lived his whole life with knowledge of this story (though no memory of it), it wasn't until he went to visit his sister's grave a few years ago that the immensity of the incident took hold for him. He was suddenly devastated and shocked by it, and began to realize how much his life had been formed around the loss. The way his parents and other siblings (who were born after the incident) treated him, the way he thought of himself—all this was conditioned, he now saw, by this event, of which he'd been barely conscious his whole life through. He began investigating the event and its implications, interviewing his parents, looking into the causes and details of the burning, rethinking his whole life with reference to it.

But after a while he realized that all of this, important as it might have been, was not getting at the real core of his concern. The psychological effects of the death were not at issue: it was the simple, awesome fact that his whole life had been shaped by an early encounter with death, and that he had never felt the force of it until now. He decided that he would begin now, so many years later, grieving for his sister, simply that. He put her picture on his home altar and said a prayer for her every day after his morning meditation. He did this for a year. During that time (his visit to the Land of the Dead), he felt things changing in his life. The coaching work he did with executives seemed to deepen. He was less interested than ever in drumming up business, networking, or starting new initiatives, but he was more interested than ever in each of his clients, and felt his capacity to meet them much increased. After the year of grieving was over he found himself in a completely different position in his life: he saw that now (he had turned sixty during the year) his life was pointing not outward into the world, as it had always done before, but rather inward toward his own emotion and reflection—and beyond. He had a new sense about how he could be living the next phase of his life.

Another friend of mine is a grief counselor and hospice chaplain, an expert on the grieving process. Being an expert on the grieving process means that you know there is no such thing as "the grieving process" because grief is different for each person. So she wasn't too surprised when she found herself completely at sea when it was her turn to grieve. Her elderly mother and father had died within a month of each other. She hadn't been very close to either of them, and, she was ashamed to admit, had been anticipating their deaths with a feeling of just wanting to get it over with, imagining that she'd probably feel very little once it happened. But the opposite was the case: her feelings were so powerful that she had to stop working, and needed a friend to move in with her just to see to it that she didn't go completely off the deep end. She felt strong feelings of guilt, terror, despair—then, seemingly in the next moment, of exaltation, liberation, joy, and then a moment later she was overwhelmed by feelings of loss and love for her parents. These contradictory rapid-fire emotional assaults exhausted her on a daily basis. It was as if the ordinary everyday world had been wiped away, and there was nothing but this immense wash of feelings that made no sense and seemed completely out of time. She feared for her sanity. When people called to offer comforting words she felt like screaming at them, "You have no idea! . . . And neither do I!" At the same time she was experiencing in her daily meditation practice a sense of peace more profound than any she had known. Each breath seemed like an eternal wave of calmness. This emotional roller coaster went on for three or four months, then gradually began to subside. When her time of grieving was over she was left feeling that all that she'd previously thought about herself (that she was an unhappy, lonely person; that she was empathetic, funny, smart) was completely wrong and that it was going to take her a long time to figure out who she actually was.

Another friend lost her father when she was a young girl. The loss devastated her and left her and her mother quite vulnerable in the world. They had a rocky time of it, and my friend ended up having many personal problems as a result of this. She knew how frightened and bewildered the untimely death of her father had made her, and how important the death had been to her formation as a person, and in her life problems, so she went to therapy and spent years dealing with the death. But she'd never in all those years visited her father's grave. When she finally did so for the first time (by now it was almost thirty years since he'd died) she was completely unprepared for what happened. It was as if a forceful wind had come blasting up from the grave to knock her down onto the ground, where she wept violently for an hour or more.

Another friend of mine is a young artist, just at the point of establishing his career. He was preparing for his first solo show in New York, at an important gallery, when at the last minute the gallery owner canceled the show. My friend had been putting so much effort into the show, and had felt so much was riding on it, that the show's cancellation completely devastated him. He felt as if the bottom was dropping out of his life. Though the gallery owner said he was canceling the show for personal reasons of his own, that it had nothing to do with my friend's work, and that he would be glad at some later time to show the work, my friend did not believe this. He was certain this story was just an excuse for the gallery owner to get rid of him in order to bring in some other artist; he was certain that this setback was the beginning of the end of his momentum toward success, and he imagined he could see a long string of failures in a descending spiral of negative energy ahead of him, ending with despair and his inability to work or earn a living. This vision was so convincing and so alarming he was on the point of going to visit the dealer to scream at him and resign forever from any involvement with him, but he managed to restrain himself from this. "My whole body was trembling uncontrollably," he told me. "I felt like an animal about to be eaten by a powerful, implacable predator. I was looking down a narrow tube of blackness and I was completely terrified."

There is no template for a visit to the Land of the Dead. It takes many forms, and its effects are various. As this last story shows, sometimes death isn't even involved: any powerful-enough loss can plunge us down to the land where the sun can't shine, where we encounter masses of terrifying shades; if we are lucky we can hold them at bay with a sword until we hear the prophecy that will enable us to go onward in our journey. And when we go on things will be different, though we can't say precisely how.

We've noted that Odysseus grows less fearful the longer he remains in the Land of the Dead. In fact, as time goes on he begins to be fascinated. He wishes he could meet many more deceased heroes like Achilles and Ajax, but just as he is beginning to feel comfortable and confident, the shades gradually increase in number, the sound of their disturbing murmuring growing louder and louder until there are hordes of them gathered about him with an inhuman clamor, and the green fear takes hold of him again with the thought that he may next be visited by a monster far more terrifying than anything he has seen so far. This terror propels him out of the Land of the Dead and back to his ships. He and his men sail away.

Though terrifying, the Land of the Dead is also, when we get a little bit used to it, fascinating. Fear can be addictive, and so can the feeling of proximity to death. Many hospice workers report an intoxicating "high" that comes with being with a patient who has just died. So it's no good for us to be too comfortable in the Land of the Dead; it is a place to visit, but not remain. Our terror of it is healthy, and we must move on.

No one chooses (at least consciously) to go to the Land of the Dead. It's natural that when we discover we have to go there we imitate Odysseus and flop down on our beds to cry our eyes out. But knowing how important, and how inevitable, the visit is, we can be ready for it when the time comes. Being with someone who is moving toward death is not a chore, it is a privilege, as anyone who has done it with open eyes and heart will attest. What would it be like to welcome those encounters when they come—or even to volunteer for them if we have the chance to do so? To take on as a spiritual practice caring for parents, friends, or loved ones when it is time to do that? Although doing so doesn't guarantee that we will make a visit to the Land of the Dead (we can be in the vicinity of the dying without actually being with them), it does make it more likely.

A meditation on death.

Begin breathing consciously, allowing the mind to quiet. Let the mind be open with gentleness and curiosity to whatever you are feeling now. If the mind hovers and flits, watch it do this.

Now focus on the following four reflections. They are obvious, you have long known them be so, but perhaps you have never contemplated them, never seriously appreciated them. Contemplate and appreciate them now. Repeat each reflection slowly, several times, pausing between each repetition to feel your inner response, whatever it is.

First, death is certain.

We know death will come, but we shrug it off, imagining it will come later, at some future indefinite date. But think: death is certain. Absolutely certain. A moment will come, just as immediate and real as this moment, when you will face the inevitable, frightening, absolute unknown.

Second, the time of death is uncertain.

Though we know that death will come we do not know when. We assume that it will come after a full life, in old age. But death often comes unexpectedly. Young people die, middle-aged people die, old people die. There are accidents, unusual diseases, sudden strokes or heart attacks. In truth, we have no idea when our time will come. Today? Tomorrow? An hour from now?

Third, you will die alone.

Though you may be fortunate to have dear ones at your bedside at the moment of death, in fact, the closer you come to death the further away they will be. As you enter the darkness—if it is darkness—you are alone.

Fourth, in death all our possessions and accomplishments are of no value. The only support for us as we die is the condition of our heart, shaped by the words, deeds, and thoughts of a lifetime.

All that has made us worthwhile people in life is useless to us in death. Death does not care if you are important or insignificant, accomplished or without skills. Have you loved? Are you kind? Is there some wisdom, forbearance, compassion in you? Only qualities like these can serve us now.

The meditation on death is not meant to depress or dismay you. It only serves to remind you of what you already know but constantly forget: that life is brief, uncertain, and precious; and that it is crucial that you tend to the quality of your heart now.

15 / The Siren Call

You'd think there would be something decisive and final about our visit to the Land of the Dead, but as we've seen, it's not so. Nothing is final; nothing is fixed. The journey of return goes on and on. Keeping patience with this is difficult, but what else can we do?

Odysseus and his men sail on doggedly. Next they must encounter the sirens, those enchanting sisters whose eerie songs irresistibly draw you in. Once in their clutches there's no escaping the doom they bring. Circe had given Odysseus instructions: he is to stop up his sailors' ears with wax as the ships sail past so the siren sound can't penetrate. If Odysseus wants to leave his own ears open, she tells him, to hear the tempting tunes, he must have his men lash him to the ship's masts, with instructions that no matter what he says he is not to be untied, and that if he asks to be untied he is to be lashed all the harder!

The story of the sirens is so much a part of our culture that we take it for granted (we all understand the term "siren song" to mean something alluring and slightly illicit). But we need to examine more closely the power of the sirens' attraction. What about their songs draws us in and dooms us forever? And why does Odysseus feel he must risk hearing them?

The sirens sing of the past, your past, my past, in this case, Odysseus' past, his many woes and his battles. And they do this in a particular way: their strange melodies, so full of pathos, sympathy, and beauty, romanticize the past; they seem to bring the struggles of yesterday back with a glow of sorrow and glory. Their songs evoke the immense, seductive power of nostalgia, of our human propensity to live in an idealized past that glosses over our ancient suffering with a patina of passionate emotion.

My father was a soldier in World War II. He fought in the artillery, and though he was close to the worst of the combat, he saw less death and was touched by less trauma than the soldiers who fought on the front lines. But he certainly experienced danger and the immense go-for-broke effort one expends in a good and desperate cause, in emotionally charged times, among close companions. As for many others of his generation, this powerful experience was probably the most intense time of my father's life, which he cherished as long as he lived. As he grew older his war experiences took on greater and greater significance. Rather than fading gradually away, they seemed instead to become more vivid. In his sixties my father loved nothing better than to get together with war buddies, to relive those days.

Although I have never been in the military, I can understand my father's feeling, because my most intense, formative experiences in monastic life were like his in the war, minus, of course, the danger and the proximity to violence. Like my father and his war buddies, my fellow monks and I were living in close, intimate contact during a highly charged, emotional period of our lives. Like them we were dedicated to a purpose beyond our personal needs, and were willing to sacrifice everything to that purpose. Like them we were a cadre apart from the world. Over the years a similar feeling of vivid nostalgia began to grow in me and my comrades as we remembered our monastic adventures. When we talk about those days now, we sound quite a bit like my father and his cronies as they spoke about their war experiences. We share feelings that seem unlike anything we have in the present. And unless someone has been through what we've been through, he cannot really understand what we feel.

I began this book with the theme of time and have been
cling back to it over and over again. How odd and strange i
to be in time, and how uncanny time is, never exactly matching
our conventional conceptions of it. Nostalgia is time supercharged
with emotion. The nostalgia-tinged past is saturated with a particular sort of emotion that is a bit too alluring. Hearing the intimate
melodies of the songs of the past, we are trapped within their mel-
low notes, and if we immerse the present moments of our lives in
these mesmerizing sounds, we will lose the unique character and
flavor of our present living. We ossify both the past and the present, as my father may have done, and as my monastic comrades
and I are probably beginning to do. Neither past nor present is
carved in stone. Both are continuously alive and marvelous, and
to fix them into a shape, however glorious that shape may be, is
to doom ourselves to become stone, too. This is the doom—and
the attraction—of the sirens. They offer a seductive, comfortable
fantasy of refuge in a past that never was, and this fantasy kills
our ongoing life. The past is crucial and unavoidable. We have to
face it, digest it, and integrate it into our present living—and this
is ongoing work. To fix and sentimentalize the past is to seal the
present's doom.

In Zen we always emphasize the "present moment." The
"present moment" is this moment, the only moment we ever live,
whose depths includes past and future as dynamic forces, without fear or nostalgia. It is not a hedonistic present that denies the
past or ignores the future. When we truly enter this moment we
feel satisfied; there's no holding on, no thirsting or longing. We
accept with appreciation whatever appears, letting go of desire
for something else—and of desire to hold on to this moment.
For as soon as the present moment arises it is gone, giving way
to a succeeding moment. In this sense, the present moment is
essentially and always a moment of renunciation, a moment of
letting go. Renunciation isn't a moral imperative or a form of
self-denial. It's simply cooperation with the way things are: for
moments do pass away, one after the other. Resisting this natural

unfolding doesn't change it; resistance only makes it painful. So we renounce our resistance, our noncooperation, our stubborn refusal to enter life as it is. We renounce our fantasy of a beautiful past and an exciting future we can cherish and hold on to. Life just isn't like this. Life, time, is letting go, moment after moment. Life and time redeem themselves constantly, heal themselves constantly, only we don't know this, and much as we long to be healed and redeemed, we refuse to recognize this truth. This is why the sirens' songs are so attractive and so deadly. They propose a world of indulgence and wishful thinking, an unreal world that is seductive and destructive.

Another related, even more insidious aspect to the sirens' songs is that they know not only the past, my past, your past, and Odysseus' past, they know everything. "No life on earth can be hid from our dreaming," they say. And this is their second powerful temptation, the temptation of knowledge, of experience.

We take it for granted that life is good, and if it is good we want more of it. We take it for granted that knowledge and experience are good, and if they are good we want more of them. Life may be good and knowledge and experience may be good, but in wanting more there is a danger. When we're always wanting more, always driving forward toward that more, we run the risk of being so caught by our addictive habit of seeking that we forget what it is to find: to find this moment, this experience, this life, enough. The traditional Buddhist discussion of suffering uses the image of a twelve-link chain of causes and conditions to illustrate what binds us to the wheel of suffering. Among these links is the desire for becoming, the desire to be more and know more. This isn't some sort of illicit or out-of-bounds lust or craving, but the normal human urge toward more life, more experience, our obsession to see, do, know more. This desire keeps us growing and learning, but it becomes a problem if we are too much caught up in it, seduced by it, so that we lose track of our center, our soul, and give ourselves over to this mania for experience. This is a danger especially for courageous, imaginative, wily people like Odysseus.

It's why Odysseus doesn't put wax in his own ears; it's why he has to, and wants to, experience the sirens' songs.

As we should, too. But, again, not without recognizing the dangers involved (the sirens' island is littered with the bones of those who did not see the danger) and not without help. Fortunately Odysseus has what he needs: a strong commitment to the journey home, and the discipline to order himself lashed to the mast; he also has a strong crew to make sure he stays lashed no matter how much he screams to be untied—which he does.

The sirens teach us valuable lessons: that our romance with the past and our urge to attain more and more knowledge and experience are both dangerous. As we learned on Circe's island, we have much within us that is excessive and perilous. Naturally, then, like Eurylochus, we become frightened and mutinous; we try to avoid or deny. But we might also go to the other extreme, as is the danger here. Rather than avoiding our desires and passions we could be seduced by them, and indulge them until they go out of bounds and doom us. Neither of these options is right. We can't avoid what's within us. No matter how dangerous it is, we need to face it and incorporate it into our journey. If we don't we'll never make it home; we'll be stuck forever on some godforsaken island, held back by what we won't face and can't acknowledge.

The sirens invite us to participate in the intoxication of the past, and in the lure of knowledge and experience. We ought to accept their invitation, but not without lashing ourselves to the mast of our spiritual discipline, and relying on our friends to keep us there when we go mad with wanting to escape. To give ourselves consciously to our journey home requires courage and risk. The way is not always safe and secure. But if we have the protections of the contemplative exercises to which we are devoted, and of our community of like-minded friends who share the journey with us, we will be able to face what we need to face without being drawn away and seduced by it and exposed to danger. With these protections we can open ourselves fearlessly (or sometimes not so fearlessly) to ourselves without being seduced or shipwrecked.

Odysseus' journey home, like ours, is neither a matter of ignoring real life nor of indulging our mania for amassing more experiences, more knowledge, or more pictures for our scrapbook. The journey home is more solid and more mysterious than that.

A basic contemplative practice.

Return once again to yourself, your true self; to breath, body, senses: to time and space. Breathe in with awareness, out with awareness. Let yourself be free and open with what arises in you, not looking for anything, not hoping for anything, not judging anything, but not denying anything either. Even if looking, hoping, and judging arise, don't worry or resist. Let them be there freely and openly, as you breathe and settle where you are.

This simple meditation practice, as I have described it many times in this book, simply being present with what we are, with the life that flows through us, guiding our every step if we will let it, is the basic contemplative exercise. All prayer, ritual, and observance come from it. Feel it now. Or add to it, if it is your practice, words of affirmation or prayer, petitions for help and support, as we have also practiced in these pages.

Remember that whenever you are fully present, with your breath and body, with your prayer or chant or ritual, you are returning to the basic sanity that has always been inside you. The spiritual journey is difficult to understand. Impossible to pin down. Sometimes dangerous, provoking great fear. But when you return to yourself (and, if you are lucky, to the community of others, near and far, living or not living, with whom you share the journey) you are protected. The wind may blow, your mind may rage, but you will be all right.

Breathe that reality in and out. Feel the strength it brings.

16 / Impossible Choices: Scylla and Charybdis

When Odysseus and his men left Circe's island, the goddess gave them precise, useful instructions, but for his next adventure Odysseus is on his own. He has no instructions to follow. He must make an impossible choice as he sails through the narrow straits of Scylla and Charybdis.

Scylla is a six-headed, twelve-limbed, sharp-toothed ravenous monster who lives in a cave halfway up a huge mountain past which the ship must sail. Constantly hungry, she strikes with all six mouths at once, snatching up six men simultaneously in her disgusting fangs from which they dangle, terrified as mice, screaming vainly for mercy. On the other side of the narrow strait is Charybdis, an even more terrifying prospect: a huge maw, a sucking endless whirlpool that appears and disappears without warning, pulling everything in its clutches down to the netherworlds below the sea. Odysseus must negotiate his way between these two horrifying obstacles, choosing which of the two he will skirt more closely.

Although this sounds like a scene from a special-effects science fiction movie, this sort of impossible choice is all too common. While we will all probably get through life without ever encountering a sucking whirlpool or a six-headed monster, none of us will escape the necessity of sailing through a narrow passage with disaster lurking port and starboard, the way through so slim that we cannot avoid the margins. There comes a time in every life when we are forced to choose between impossible alternatives. My business friends frequently share with me the impossible choice they sometimes face in business decisions: should they do what seems most ethical, though it will negatively affect the bottom line, or should they relax their moral standard in order to capture immediate profits. While this might seem to nonbusinesspeople an easy decision, businesspeople know it's not: the ethical imperative to stay in business, in order to employ people who are supporting families and to serve customers' and stockholders' needs, must also be taken into account when weighing the morality of any business decision. Sometimes in business it gets worse than this, though: you are forced to choose between two clearly unethical alternatives. How long can you sustain such choices?

In love one often faces an impossible choice between leaving a long-standing troubled relationship, with all its entanglements, obligations, and history, or trying to improve it, despite the mutually destructive habits of interaction between the partners that seem set in stone. Families face horrible, unsatisfactory choices when a loved one grows old, feeble, and incompetent, or when that same relative lies in a coma on life support. I faced just such a gut-wrenching impossible choice at the time of my father's death, when it was up to me to decide whether to leave him on the breathing machine, or take him off. Women sometimes face an impossible choice when it is up to them to decide, sometimes without advice or support, whether or not to end an unwanted or possibly dangerous pregnancy. Impossible choices are daily and normal for soldiers in wartime.

In all these situations there is no way to make a good choice—and no way not to choose. When I was a young man I used to imagine that the moral choice was always possible if only one were courageous enough. Once one of my Zen teachers, sensing my naïveté, posed a problem for me. One of two people is to be shot by a firing squad. One is a teenage boy who is ill with a serious disease. The other is his mother, who is well. One must die and one will live. The authorities require you to choose. Which do you choose? "There is no way to choose," I said. "I would not choose." "You must choose!" he shouted at me.

Sometimes spiritual matters are discussed in a cut-and-dried manner, as though there were clear principles, and one need only follow these principles, whose application is always precise, and all will be well. But life isn't theoretical, theological, or precise, and things are not usually as simple and as clear as we would like them to be. Sometimes all the available choices are bad. Sometimes you are caught in the grip of circumstances beyond your control. You have to do something, whatever you do will be wrong, and you will have to live with the consequences.

The question of life choices has other drastic aspects. Sometimes the problem is not choosing bad alternatives, but that there is really no choice: the passage is not a passage through but a passage down into hell and you are sucked into it, with no way out. You are paralyzed, frozen, as you face the abyss. I have a friend who, like many, has sailed down this black hole. He's Mexican, living an ordinary—but a painfully lonely—life in Mexico City. For years he coped with his loneliness with alcohol, which worked well, up to a point. But eventually he found the alcohol was ruining him. He was more isolated than ever, his health was beginning to fail him, but he was powerless to stop drinking. He felt himself at a point of no return, with no exit, no option. He didn't know what to do, where to turn. To go on as he was was impossible; to find a different way to go was equally impossible. He was sinking fast.

A friend of his who was religious suggested that, under the circumstances, perhaps he was ready to go to church, talk to a priest, attend Mass, or, if he didn't feel comfortable with that, just go and sit in a church and ask God for help in whatever way he could. Not a churchgoer, my friend was, in fact, a committed socialist and atheist, who had long felt that religion was nothing more than a tool used by the rich to keep the poor downtrodden. For years he had espoused this doctrine, and was proud of the fact that he had absolutely no need for the superstitious comfort that religion offers to the gullible. Still, there was nowhere else to go and nothing else to do so the next day he went to the nearest church. It was closed. So he went to another, and then another and another—all closed. Finally, more despondent than desperate, he sat down on a bench outside of one of the churches and simply wept.

In this state of complete collapse he found himself asking out loud for help, just as my Zen friend had done. Whom he was asking he didn't know. It wasn't God; he didn't believe in that; the word *God* was ash in his mouth. And then, suddenly, as if a warm breeze had caressed him, melting and relaxing his soul, he was overcome with a feeling of certainty that he had been answered. He felt with tremendous clarity that his call for help had been answered. There was no particular answer, no flash of insight. But he felt that his cry had been met by an outward force beyond him. This feeling affected his body immediately. He felt physically as if he were being opened from inside. His body felt held, cradled. He looked around, blinking his eyes as if he were looking at the world for the first time. Everything looked different. The trees were a greener green. The flowers seemed conscious, as if they were looking intentionally at him. From that day his life changed. He began a recovery program that has continued to the present. I heard him tell this story sixteen years after it happened, and when he told it his arms were covered with goosebumps and his face glowed with pleasure.

Impossible choices. No choice. And sometimes profound choices you didn't know you'd made. Sometimes the problem is that you have chosen a life without realizing that you've done this, that you have passed through Scylla and Charybdis and incurred great losses of which you were not aware. You feel beaten, oppressed, stuck, and you don't see that you've brought this state on yourself, that you actually chose it. When you finally recognize that you have made a choice, and take responsibility for that, you feel free.

This is what another friend of mine learned from an encounter with her Buddhist teacher. A passionate social activist, also in Mexico, my friend has been doing battle for years with local authorities on behalf of the poor people in her region. Local politics in Mexico can be fairly complicated and fairly brutal, and my friend has had to be very tough, sometimes even ruthless, just to survive. But she has survived, and has managed to earn a reputation as a force to be reckoned with in her town. Of course this hasn't been easy for her. Her passion for justice has served her well in one way: it has made her fierce and unrelenting in the service of others. But it has also worn her out, discouraged her sometimes, and often given rise to strong anger that has had bad effects on her physical and psychological well-being. In the hope that it would bring her some peace, she took up meditation practice.

In a meditation retreat with her Vietnamese teacher, she sat for long hours on her cushion unable to focus her mind. All she could do was review the many disputes and fights in which she had been involved over the years of her political activism. The scenes went on and on, and kept speeding up in her mind, with more and more passion. As the days of the long retreat wore on, sitting on her meditation cushion she was becoming more and more angry at her opponents, at the Mexican government in general, and at the world for its persistent, virulent injustice. Finally, when it was time to go to see the teacher to talk about her practice, she was in a fury. During the retreat the teacher had been talking constantly about peace. She strode into his quiet, incense-scented room and shouted, "I don't want peace—I want justice!" The teacher quietly replied, "Difficult choice." At this my friend was thunderstruck. She had been an activist since adolescence but it had never occurred to her that that had been a choice—an impossible choice to fight against injustice in an unjust world. Hearing the teacher's words she saw that it was a choice, one that she had freely made.

Somehow the words illuminated her: she recognized that the world was what it was, she was who she was, and that she was free, and had always been free, not bound, to fight the fight she had been fighting. She walked out of the interview room as if on a cloud. Like the man on the church bench, she felt as if her body had opened up, and she saw the world brighter, lighter, and more beautiful. Since that day she has continued with her activism. It is still difficult sometimes, but never as difficult as it had been before she understood that she has chosen to do it, however impossible a choice it may be.

Let's practice with this question of choices.

Imagine Scylla and Charybdis. You need not create a six-headed monster or a sucking whirlpool. It is enough to feel the surging sea, the whirling waves that crash against the steep walls of a jagged rocky canyon. You know that sailing through this narrow passage will be difficult. How will you steer your boat?

Take time now to meditate on the choices—conscious and unconscious—that have shaped your life. Don't be too quick to do this. The choices that spring to mind right away may not be the most salient ones. So begin by clearing your mind, opening your heart, and waiting to see what comes. Notice how you feel as thoughts or images come and go.

Think of the choices you are conscious of having made. Can you imagine choices you may have made unconsciously? Do you have regrets? Would you have chosen differently, if you could?

Did you ever experience a time when it seemed that there was no choice at all? If you did, was this a desperate, hemmed-in feeling? Or was it liberating to feel that you had no choice but to go ahead with your destiny, as if it had been decided in advance by superior powers?

Did you ever face a moral dilemma? What did you do? Was what you did right? Was it wrong? How easy is it to say?

How do you feel about close friends, or those more distant—say political or business leaders—and the moral choices you imagine they have faced? Does considering your own choices help you to appreciate theirs in a new way?

Odysseus chooses Scylla. In spite of Circe's warning, he imagines he can defeat the monster. Directing the ships near her cliff, he draws his sword, but she snatches six of his men and devours them as he looks on, hopeless. "That was the most pitiful scene that these eyes have looked on in my sufferings as I explored the routes over the water," Odysseus says as he tells the tale to the Phaiakians.[1] But in spite of these losses he has avoided the loss of all his ships and men to Charybdis, the whirlpool.

Odysseus next sails to the island of Thrinakia, where the sacred cattle of Helios, the sun god, graze. Odysseus has been warned not to slaughter these cattle under any circumstances, and not to allow his men to do so, for the consequences would be disastrous. With all that has happened already, Odysseus is loathe to land here, for fear of what might go wrong, but his men plead for a short respite before sailing on. Making the men swear that they will not touch the sacred cows, come what may, Odysseus agrees to the stop. But just as they are ready to vacate the island, the winds disappear, the boats can't sail, and the short sojourn stretches on for a month. Food runs out. The men are starving. Odysseus goes off by himself deep into the forest to make offerings and pray for good weather. And there he does what he so often has done at crucial moments (and, I am afraid, what we also so often do when in our journey matters become sticky or intractable): he falls asleep. And, again, Odysseus' slumber leads to disaster. The ever-persuasive, ever-mutinous Eurylochus incites the men to break their oath. It's better to take our chances with the gods than starve to death, he says. They slaughter the sacred cattle.

Odysseus, returning, is aghast at what they have done. But it's too late now. They feast, a wind comes up, and they hastily sail away. But they encounter almost immediately a fierce thunderbolt-driven storm. It blasts their ship to pieces. All the men perish in the icy seas. Only Odysseus is left alive. He clings to a makeshift raft as the currents draw him inexorably back—yes, all the way back to Charybdis. So it seems that, inadvertently, he has chosen both bad alternatives. The awful sucking whirlpool swallows the pitiful raft. Odysseus saves himself at the last minute by clutching onto the branch of a fig tree clinging to the mountain suspended over the abyss. He dangles there for a very long time (as long, the text says, as a lawyer waits for all the cases at court to finish). When finally Charybdis disgorges a single splintered piece of the raft, Odysseus lets loose and falls onto it, exhausted. On this splintered log, alone, half drowned, Odysseus floats toward Ogygia, where he will remain for seven years with the goddess Calypso— where our story began.

Many themes emerge from this final series of disasters. First and most noticeable is the recurrence of complaints, rebellion, mutiny, the great common theme of all who undertake the physical and metaphoric journey home. One of our perennial issues on the journey is our ambivalence: as Samuel Beckett puts it, we must go on, we can't go on. In the episode of the Aeolian winds, ambivalence led to fatigue and then to slumber. With Odysseus asleep the men rebelled, and the consequences were disastrous. The challenge of the cattle of Helios involves the same elements: fatigue and sleepiness, complaining and rebellion. If we haven't gotten it before, the pattern by now is all too clear: our intractable human confusion and resistance keep sabotaging us. Despite our best intentions and all our skill and determination, and even with our spiritual practice and guidance, something within us, something we can't seem to shake or even to see, keeps on making sure that our journey home will be long and difficult—exactly as long and as difficult (and repetitive!) as it needs to be.

In the whining of Odysseus' men I hear an echo of the biblical story of the exodus from Egypt. In that tale, the children of Israel, after their dramatic, miraculous escape through the parted waters of the Red Sea, almost immediately take to complaining bitterly to Moses about the hardships of the wilderness. The story of their rebellion occupies much of the rest of the Five Books of Moses. How true to life this is. How often the miracle of release and salvation leads very quickly to dissatisfaction, ingratitude, and complaining. You can almost count on it. When Zen students tell me about some breakthrough they have had, on the meditation cushion, in life, or both, I am always delighted for them. But I also know that this big moment is not the end of the story. The journey is not over yet, not by a long shot. There will certainly be surprising, devastating disasters still to come, and very quickly the moment of accomplishment and joy gives way to uncomfortable, inconvenient events, and then, naturally, to disappointment and complaining.

In the story of our journey home we are Odysseus and Moses. We go off to the mountaintop to pray, where, perhaps, we fall asleep (like Odysseus), unless (as with Moses) our attention is occupied with a fierce encounter with the transcendent. Either way, we are not out of the woods, because we are not only Odysseus and Moses. We are also Odysseus' crew and the children of Israel, a mutinous band of whining, contradictory passions, who will, in the temporary absence of our better selves (asleep or God-occupied), sabotage our own noblest efforts.

Benedict, the great saint whose fourth-century Rule regulates Christian monasteries to this day, used the word *murmuring* to refer to the complaining of the children of Israel in the wilderness, the habitual human complaining that seems to be a normal feature of the journey of return. The word *murmuring* is repeated over and over again in his Rule. For, it seems, monks in monasteries, like children on long car rides, and like us as we stumble through life, also complain quite a bit. It's certainly true in Zen monasteries, at least in the West, where monastics are always complaining that it is too hot, too cold, too early, too late, and the food is too spicy or not spicy enough. Such "murmuring" is one of the great problems of the spiritual life, and of life in general. There is always plenty to complain about and most of us are not shy about expressing ourselves when it comes to things that annoy us.

While murmuring may have a bad name, and lead more often than not to bad consequences, as we see in *The Odyssey* and the Bible, it is quite understandable. It may not be entirely a bad thing. It is human to complain. Besides, as we saw with Telemachus in the assembly, sometimes it is necessary to speak your grief, to give voice to all your troubles and frustrations. Saint Benedict aside, murmuring can be salubrious and provide psychological relief, providing we know how to do it in the proper way, without getting tangled up in it, which is what happens when we take ourselves too seriously. If we can sing or dance or paint or laugh our complaints, they might serve us well enough, freeing us from our misery at least for a while, and allowing others to commiserate with us and appreciate our difficulty. Complaining out loud might relieve our loneliness and the tension of an otherwise grim situation, providing we don't rush out, as a consequence of our complaining, and manufacture a golden calf—or eat one.

And here we come to an important if subtle crux: the disaster of the cattle of Helios is caused precisely by eating. Odysseus' men eat what ought not to be eaten. The cattle of Helios (like everything in this world, inside and out) are sacred. As such, they require that we appreciate, protect, and engage them rather than devour them. In the cattle of Helios, I hear another biblical echo: the fruit in the garden of Eden, which was to be recognized and appreciated, but under no circumstances eaten. Just as it was inevitable that Odysseus' men would eat the cattle of Helios, and that Adam and Eve would eat the forbidden fruit, so it is inevitable that we will eat what is sacred in our own lives. Doing this will cause, as in the mythic stories that we read as counterpoint and commentary to our life narratives, an unavoidable series of disasters. And these disasters will be our pathway home. Although Adam and Eve's feasting is called "sin," a close, sensitive reading of the text will show in fact that it was necessary and even expected. Yes, Adam and Eve have free will; they made a choice. And yet their choice was also part of the divine plan. How else could the rest of the story unfold if this seminal event had not happened? Milton's *Paradise Lost* makes the Christian perspective on this clear: that Jesus appears because Adam and Eve eat; the salvation he brings requires their sin. Likewise, although the eating of the cattle of Helios led to a great tragedy, it is precisely by virtue of this tragedy that Odysseus could advance to his eventual return. The rhyme with our own lives is clear: we eat what we should not eat, disaster ensues, and it is just the disaster we need. How can we understand more carefully this destructive human eating? Again our great guide Simone Weil has something useful to say:

"The great trouble in human life," she tells us, "is that looking and eating are two different operations. Only beyond the sky, in the country inhabited by God, are they one and the same operation. Children feel this trouble already when they look at a cake for a long time almost regretting that it should have to be eaten and yet unable to help eating it. . . . Eve began it. If she caused humanity to be lost by eating the fruit, the opposite attitude, looking at the fruit without eating it, should be what is required to save it. 'Two winged companions,' says an Upanishad, 'two birds are on the branch of a tree. One eats the fruit the other looks at it.' These two birds are the two parts of our soul."[2]

In this passage Weil touches on what the whole of this second part of *The Odyssey* has been leading us toward. It explains the underlying cause of all the disasters that life keeps perpetrating on us. When we appreciate our experience as it is, engaging with it fully, but not trying to possess or control it—looking but not eating—then whatever life throws our way will be all right. We can look to our heart's content, we can even complain all we want, but if we don't eat—don't, that is, swallow Circe's potion without a counterpotion, or listen to the sirens' songs without being lashed to the mast, but instead appreciate and move on for the rest of the journey—then we avert disaster. Sometimes this is the way it ought to be. But there are other times, as with the sacred cattle, the lotus blossoms, and the Cyclopes' food, when we can't help but eat, to our great sorrow. Disasters ensue, and we must find a way out of them. This is no simple matter of dos and don'ts, right and wrong actions. It is not an either-or proposition. We are not simply supposed to forgo eating the fruit and the cattle, or swallowing the potion, or allowing ourselves to be seduced by sound and sight: of course we need to do these things, we are human, we eat to live, and we must pay the price of our eating. This also is our destiny, and our path home.

Adventures born of disaster are always in store for us. But they flow from our essential soul. They add interest, color, and texture to the journey. They also test us, teach us, and make us strong enough to make it all the way back home again. Redemption requires that we first fall. Odysseus returns to Ithaca only after long struggle. We come home only after leaving and getting into trouble. Note that the Upanishad says there are two parts to our soul—not a good part and a bad part, an acceptable part and a rejectable part, but simply two parts. Both must be honored. One brings us disaster. One saves us. Both are necessary.

But questions remain: Is there a way to appreciate without eating? What would this mean and how could we live in this way? How do we work with the passion and energy of our human experience? How do we hold it and live it without being seduced more than we ought to be or entangled more than we can sustain?

As is by now abundantly clear, the journey of return is not a walk through a park. It requires us to confront everything inside us, much of which is neither pleasant not simple. We must make room for all our denial, all our passion, our fear, our ambivalence. None of it can be avoided. All of it is perilous. There's no way to protect ourselves from ourselves, to be invulnerable to what life will evoke within us. Nor would we want to. But we need a way to hold it all so that we can appreciate it, make use of it, engage it creatively, and stay on course without being entirely and finally smashed against the shoals. How can we experience the fullness of our living without flinching? How can we open to the strong emotions we will encounter on the journey without being swallowed up by them? How do we negotiate our disasters, keep them from doing us in entirely, so that we can stay afloat?

When we reflected on the episode with the sorcerer goddess Circe, we began to discuss the Buddhist practice of working with emotions. We said then that Buddhism advises us to be honest with our emotions, and to develop a spacious enough inner life to be able to appreciate fully the whole range of our emotional life and even express it without being harmed by it, or harming others. Now is the time to go into this more thoroughly, because at this point it is clear that the way we approach our emotional life is not adjunct to the journey home, something that will make the journey more or less pleasant: it *is* the journey. Looking back at all we have seen and said so far, it is obvious that the journey of return—the spiritual journey home that we are all on, whether we want to be or not—is an emotional journey, a journey of deep feeling, one that will require a more thorough and acute understanding and appreciation of what our emotions are, and what place they occupy in the overarching economy of our inner lives.

In her landmark work on emotions, *Upheavals of Thought,* philosopher Martha Nussbaum points out that Western culture has marginalized emotion by identifying it with a negative conception of the feminine, with, that is, all that is messy, inexact, troublesome, and uncontrollable in human life. Emotion, our culture assumes, is automatic, visceral, irrational, animal-like, something we need to be civilized out of. The "masculine" virtues of will, intellect, rationality, and morality are opposed to emotion and ought to rule over it. These virtues are to be cultivated so that our base emotional nature can eventually be overridden and the passions made to serve higher ends. Nussbaum proposes that this traditional bias is completely wrong, and has led to a severe destructive imbalance in Western culture. In reality, she says, there is no firewall between emotion and intellect. Emotions are not messy destructive passions to be overcome by intellect, reason, and morality. They are "upheavals of thought," no more separable from will and intellect than a crease is separable from a sheet of paper or a wave from the ocean. There is no emotion without thought, and no thought without emotion. To repress emotion with intellect and will is to do violence to our human nature. We need not fear and flee from emotion so much as understand, appreciate, and integrate it into a whole life, she proposes.[3]

Nussbaum's view is supported by the traditional Buddhist conception of mind. In Buddhist psychology, consciousness and object arise together. When they meet, a field of experience is activated that includes various subjective elements classified in a number of ways. Consciousness always includes some awareness, some thought, some perception, some reactivity from the past, some overarching attitude and some impulse to action. Such elements combine in complex ways to produce what we might call thoughts and emotions, but Buddhist psychology makes no important distinction between thought, emotion, or will (they are all just subjective elements arising), nor is there any sense of a hierarchy of mental or emotional states. For Buddhism the only important distinction is whether or not there is an accurate awareness and nonclinging acceptance of the flow of subjective experience. "Suffering" is inaccurate awareness of subjective experience so that you get stuck to experiences and twist them around until they become painful and harmful. For Buddhism the destructive passions are not automatic and natural; they are the result of this sticking to experiences and twisting them based on an inaccurate awareness of what is going on. "Awakening" is the opposite of this. With an accurate awareness, there is the overcoming of the sticking and twisting so that experiences can flow freely. For Buddhism, emotion, intellect, will, morality, rationality are all simply interrelating elements of consciousness that arise and pass away. None of them is more or less important in its own right. For Buddhism, you might say, allowing the free flow of emotional experience is the practice and the goal.

The focus, then, of the Buddhist practice of working with emotions is to allow emotions to arise with as accurate an awareness of them as possible, and without sticking or twisting. This is most easily done in meditation practice, but once we train on our meditation cushions, we can continue the cultivation all the time until finally there is no special sense of cultivation but simply living life as a fully feeling person.

In discussing meditation in this book I've said that meditation is essentially just sitting in the present moment of our being alive. We do create a focus for our mind to return to (awareness of the breath and of the posture) as anchor, but the point is not that we fiercely cling to that focus, but rather that we use it to help us avoid the sticking and twisting of thought and emotion that has become so habitual for us. Left to our own devices, and without any technique, the chances are overwhelming that we will not be able to avoid this sticking and twisting, which we have come to accept uncritically as the normal ordinary functioning of our hearts. But with meditation on breathing and the body we will little by little unstick and untwist ourselves. We will find sufficient calmness, stability, and spaciousness to be able to allow ourselves to feel what we are actually feeling (rather than censoring our feelings, so that we don't actually feel them, which is one result of the sticking and twisting). We will be able to let the feelings (and thoughts, for thoughts and feelings are always associated with one another and cannot really be separated) come and go without dismay or confusion, knowing that we are strong enough to bear any thought that might arise, and, in any case, that a feeling does not necessarily have to lead to an action. We can just let whatever arises come and go and it is all right. We can entertain thought and feeling without indulging it. We can appreciate it without eating it.

In many of the preceding meditations I have been asking you to practice in this way. You can practice it again now by being with your breath, body, and heart-mind with a gentle permissive openness: Observe whatever arises and subsides. Acknowledge and release. See and let go.

Having the capacity simply to be aware of mental states coming and going can be quite instructive. For instance, if a strong emotion arises in response to an event or an encounter of some kind, you see that there is a powerful immediate impulse to act: to burst out with word or deed. But if you can resist that, and instead remain intimately aware of the feeling, other things come into view. Sometimes you ascertain other feelings, thoughts, or memories that were lurking behind the initial feeling. And sometimes, if you can be fiercely aware with the feeling (and awareness does not mean analysis, it means to be present with) so that you do not get carried away by it but simply stay close with it, to the point where you become the feeling, and are not separate from it, then you will see that even in the middle of a fiercely painful feeling like searing anger or lustful desire, there is a point of purity. This is surprising but true. In the middle of anger you can see the passion for justice, a strong energy for the good; in the middle of lust you can see selfless love. It's as if by keeping your gaze steady you have been able to see to the bottom of the feeling, through the turbulent waters caused by your stickiness, to the calm clear depth.

One of my favorite lines in Zen literature, one that I constantly practice and often refer to, is found in eighteenth Century Japanese Zen master Torei Enji's poem "Bodhisattva Vow." Torei writes of following every moment's flash of thought and feeling to its end, where, he says, "You will find a lotus blossom, and on every blossom sits a Buddha." This line is important to me because once in deep meditation I saw its profound truth: Every thought, every feeling, no matter how mixed up or illicit it may seem, is wise at bottom (if you can get to the bottom, can hold firm that long). Every thought, every feeling, has some Buddha message for you, if only you can get close enough to listen.

Usually we can't get that close. We take the thought or feeling at face value, and off we go impulsively, with our hurt or desire, our denial or our misunderstanding. But if you can stay close you will see the lotus blossom at the end of the thought or feeling, with the Buddha seated on it, and you will appreciate your feelings much more, no matter what they are. And you will trust them, and be willing to allow them, without getting caught by them so easily. With this trust, you will no longer feel the need to deny or overcome or override your feelings. You will see that you can learn from them, and that they can be reliable guides. Your feelings will become more fluid and more beautiful and you will feel them more deeply. Feelings that have always been yours, but in the past perhaps arose only on rare or dramatic occasions—like love, compassion, aesthetic appreciation, gratitude—will become more frequent, even ordinary. Empathy will increase so that you will feel with others. Through the practice of working with feelings in this way you will have transformed your relationship to them.

Traditional Western thought doesn't consider that such transformation is possible. It assumes that we will all react more or less the same way to particular sorts of stimulation (barring of course severe trauma, which distorts our feeling), and that these human reactions are a given of human nature. If, for instance, someone cuts you off in traffic, anger will arise; if someone pays you a compliment, you will feel flattered and pleased. And any of us would feel such things in such cases. The question is, how good is our impulse control: do we smash into the car in front of us or do we restrain ourselves; do we fawn and preen over the compliment or do we take it in stride. It is my impression that Western psychology, until recently, has not proposed a positive vision of emotional health or emotional beauty that one might aspire to. Until the fairly new positive psychology movement, the science was rooted in its medical origins as a path toward curing pathology by proposing ways to heal severe emotional wounding.

Buddhism, and any spiritual path that will truly take us on the journey home, wants to take us beyond the mere prevention of emotional pathology. It assumes that our emotional life is not a given, and that our goal, the spiritual journey of return, proposes nothing less than the radical transformation of our emotional life so that we are no longer subject to cramped, often painful emotions that make our lives small. Instead we open ourselves to a life in which we can feel fully with the whole world in a spontaneous, harmonious, and lovely way. The awakening promised by Buddhism and other deep spiritual paths is much more than mental health, emotional normalcy. In Zen's version of the story of the Buddha's sudden illumination the great sage exclaims, "How marvelous! How marvelous! I and all things awaken in this moment!" When we finally come home to ourselves, in the truest sense, the whole world brightens and opens like a lotus.

The Dalai Lama is often taken to be the paradigmatic Buddhist practitioner, and is well loved as such. In *Destructive Emotions,* a book edited by Daniel Goleman that records a conference with the Dalai Lama and Western scientists on working with emotions, there's a wonderful description of the Dalai Lama's face. Though he is now over seventy years old, the Dalai Lama's smooth facial muscles resemble those of a twenty-year-old, no doubt because he is such a beautifully feeling person, easily experiencing and expressing, without occlusion, a range of human emotions in an ongoing flow. Most people repress their feelings and do not trust and accept the bounty of their own hearts. We are so often unaware of our feelings; or, when we are aware of them, we are shamed or embarrassed by them; or we think that our feelings are inappropriate or socially unacceptable, and try to keep from feeling them; or we try to avoid showing our feelings in our facial expressions. By contrast, the Dalai Lama seems free and natural with what he feels. He must have a tremendous sense of trusting his own heart, and a great deal of tolerance for himself and for others. It would be good if we could all, like him, know that our feelings were not merely willful, selfish, and small, but that we could rely on them to arise out of our highest aspirations and intentions, shaped by our long training on the spiritual path.

All the stories we have been considering—of Circe, the sirens, the Cyclopes, the Aeolian winds, the Land of the Dead, Scylla and Charybdis, and the cattle of Helios—have been flashbacks, recalled by Odysseus as he sits feasting at the banquet thrown for him by the good king Alcinous on Skeria. Odysseus landed on Skeria after leaving Ogygia and Calypso's arms. King Alcinous and the rest of the Phaiakian nobility are so impressed with Odysseus' amazing, colorful tale that they shower him with praise and gifts—so many gifts that he has more booty now than he'd lost at sea. Laden down with these gifts, and escorted by the expert Phaiakian sailors, Odysseus sets sail at last for Ithaca, land of his birth, his sweet home and final destiny.

And so, after seven long years of confinement on Ogygia, which followed three years of disastrous wandering, after ten years of fighting at Troy, Odysseus is finally about to return home. The ship surges on, swiftly reaching the windswept shores of Ithaca, long the subject of Odysseus' dreams and passions. And now (could it be so?) Odysseus is about to arrive. The emotion of it is more than he can bear. It floods his heart, producing a light so bright he is blinded. And so Odysseus lands on Ithaca not as a conqueror, or a pilgrim, or a king: he arrives like a baby or one as yet unborn—he arrives sound asleep, for the power of his emotion has produced such fatigue in him he cannot remain conscious. He must be carried ashore by the Phaiakian crew, and gently laid down under an olive tree. After all that's happened by now it might be safe to assume that, home at last, the worst is over. But that would be incorrect. For the real, decisive battle is now about to be joined.

Part Three

Return

After long trial, we find the courage to
meet our life—and others—face-to-face

"So the suitors lay in heaps, corpse covering
corpse."

—*The Odyssey*[1]

17 / Sleep

Ah, sleep! As we've seen several times before, the sudden onset of sleep at crucial moments usually spells disaster for Odysseus. Sleep is unawareness, unconsciousness, oblivion, a complete lack of attention. When Odysseus falls asleep, his men (who represent, most of the time, his lower impulses) are free to act (to open the bag of winds, to slaughter the sacred cattle) and severe trouble ensues. Buddhist practice and religious practice in general place a high premium on being "awake," meaning having awareness. We are enjoined always to be aware of what we are doing, so that we can align our actions with our highest intentions, and guard ourselves against our basest intentions. When Odysseus falls asleep, he fails to be aware.

Buddhist meditation is, in its most basic form, the cultivation of awareness or vigilance, usually called mindfulness. It begins with awareness of the body and the breath, and extends to awareness of emotions, thoughts, and actions. The Buddha recommended mindfulness as "the single way to deliverance," claiming that it and it alone would lead the practitioner to happiness and the end of all anguish. In my discussion of meditation at the close of part one, I explained how simply sitting in stillness, being aware of the present moment of your sitting and breathing, sets in motion a powerful force in your living. Following the thread of mindfulness gives you deeper access to your inner life and more skillfulness in dealing with it. Being asleep in your life—sleep being the precise opposite of mindfulness—is definitely a problem, as Odysseus has seen to his great sorrow, and as you have no doubt seen, too. Recall the shocks you have had when you've suddenly realized how unaware you've been of what's been going on with a relationship, your health, your emotions and, one day, you awakened to a disastrous situation that you had no idea had been brewing for some time. So, yes, mindfulness is key, but, as with everything that takes place on the journey home, all rules are subject to revision. Nothing is always so. If we look a bit more deeply we will see another side to sleep.

Think about it: the path of each and every day necessarily leads to sleep. We need to sleep, to rest. We need to be unconscious, unaware, oblivious, for some time every day. Spiritual practice, our life's journey home, is more than a faith or a technique or a set of good intentions that we can hold up to the light of our conscious minds; certainly it's more mysterious than that. In our sleep, deep within our unconscious resting, something is going on. Every night, our spiritual selves, our journeying selves, advance, develop, and deepen in the dark openness that unconsciousness and a lack of intention afford. Who knows what realms we travel in our dreams, what adventures we endure or enjoy, what problems we face? Who knows how we mix up time and identity as we lie on our pillows? In the morning we wake, sometimes refreshed, sometimes confused, sometimes slightly disoriented, usually without much knowledge of where we have been or what has gone on in our slumbers.

Sleep can be frustrating and frightening. Sometimes, when our inner journeying brings us to the narrow passage between the horrors of Scylla and Charybdis, or causes us to be held captive on an island where we remain pleasantly stagnant for a long while, we feel so much pent-up anxiety that sleep becomes difficult, if not impossible, desperate as our need for it may be. We call this restlessness insomnia, that awful condition in which our minds refuse to turn off, insisting instead on racing around and around through the night with cascades of thinking and feeling, most of it unpleasant, even fearful. And when we don't sleep at night, our days have a way of going out of focus; they slip away from us, and we become increasingly afraid of the trouble that might come as a result of our physical exhaustion and psychic depletion. Our anxiety level mounts day by day. Long before bedtime we begin dreading the night. We visit doctors, take medications, try whatever remedies we can find, but none of them works; they only seem to feed the beast of our sleeplessness.

Have you ever noticed how some children have a natural aversion to sleep, as if anticipating this particularly adult dilemma? From an early age they resist it mightily. I was that sort of child, and I well remember the great difficulties my parents had getting me to bed every night, and how, once I was there, I'd sneak out as soon as I could to lurk in the darkened hallway where I could listen to the murmur of the grown-ups' conversations. When I was caught out and put back into bed I'd stubbornly lie awake as long as I could. I'd often wake up in the morning with the sensation that I'd never slept at all, which was why I was convinced that I didn't need to sleep, because I thought I hardly ever did.

In my case it was the fear of missing something rather than the fear of sleeping itself that disturbed me (or so it seemed). But many children are afraid of sleep. And probably adults are, too. They feel a terror of darkness and fear the letting go into unconsciousness that sleep requires: for in sleep we are not in control, we are at the mercy of whatever demons lurk inside us. And, perhaps worse than this, sleep cuts off our conscious life. There is some deep dread here, too, for how can we be assured that consciousness will return to us in the morning? The experience of sleep, as philosophers have often remarked, is perilously close to the experience of dying, and so, though we know we need to do it (just as we know we need to die), something in us resists. I wonder how many people over the last several generations have been permanently scarred by that old childhood bedtime prayer that includes the line "if I should die before I wake"? Some fearful demon in us prefers not to test the hypothesis that sleeping always ends in waking. A strange, eerie feeling comes with being awake in the middle of the night, when everyone else is asleep and we know we should be, too. We are in a state that is not exactly wakefulness but certainly isn't sleep, a state in which the realities of the daytime fade and the much more ominous realities of the night prevail. Sleep and insomnia are the province of ghosts and nightmares.

It cannot be a coincidence that all the great contemplative traditions schedule spiritual exercises in the early morning hours, usually before dawn. At the Zen Center we'd usually begin to meditate at about 5 A.M., except during monastic training periods, when we'd start at 4 or sometimes earlier. I always thought of that as being rather early until I went to practice at Gethsemane Abby, Thomas Merton's Trappist monastery in Kentucky, where the early morning office began at about 3.

Many people wonder what's so special about early morning for prayer or meditation. Isn't any time of day as good? Isn't there something perversely self-denying about getting up so early, interrupting a good sleep? Besides, aren't we all groggy and still half asleep at three o'clock in the morning? If the point of spiritual endeavor is the cultivation of awareness and conscious intention for the good, why not undertake this when we are fully awake and alert, after, say, toast and coffee?

But the truth is, very early morning really is a better time for spiritual practice. For one thing, it's always quiet, both inside and outside, even in a busy city. When neither we nor the world is yet fully awake we are more vulnerable and therefore more open to spiritual influences. As Merton puts it, "The dawn is by its very nature a peaceful, mysterious, and contemplative time of day, a time when one naturally pauses and looks with awe at the Eastern sky."[1]

But another reason the very early morning (or, one might say, the middle of the night) is such a good time for spiritual practice is that getting up very early interrupts our dreams, which forces us to bring them with us to our spiritual practice. When we arise before our dreams can fully occur and go quickly to our meditation cushions or prayer benches, we allow the liminal mind of the dream world to act itself out in our meditation practice. And so our early morning practice is—as it is in monasteries the world over—dreamy practice, not quite awake and not quite asleep. This seems to be quite different from the clarity and control we associate with awareness, with the bright awakeness of the Buddha, and in a way it is.

But clarity is probably overrated. After all, isn't it our much-vaunted clarity that got us into spiritual trouble in the first place? With clarity we launched forth into our life of plans and schemes, building a great citadel that ended up crushing us. And then, possibly, we brought that same mind-set, that same clear desiring and calculating mind, into our spiritual endeavor, as if we could draw up a plan for spiritual success, complete with timelines and objectives. Perhaps it's less, not more, clarity that we need. Zen Master Zhaozho once said, "As soon as you know enough to say something you have clarity. But I am not clear."[2] Perhaps rather than trusting so much in clarity, and thinking of sleep and unawareness as enemies, we need to trust them more as allies. Although we don't know what goes on in our dreams, perhaps we need to trust them anyway as our best, wisest partners on the way. As Zen Master Dogen writes, "The Dharma [Truth] is a dream within a dream."[3]

The lineage of spiritual dreaming goes back very far. In medieval Japan the great monks Keizan and Myoe (who kept a detailed dream diary for more than thirty years) were both guided by their dreams and visions. All cultures have recognized the prophetic power inherent in dreams. The Bible is full of tales of dreams and their power. Jacob's dream of the ladder that is rooted in earth but ascends to heaven, up and down which angels move, is the first strong hint he has that, as he says, "God was in this place but I didn't know it." And later he dreams (or is it a dream?—the text presents it as a waking vision) of a "strange man" he wrestles with all night long, a man who, in departing, gives him his true, new name, Israel, the one who struggles with God. Joseph appears as a dream interpreter, and this skill not only gets him released from prison, it also results in his appointment as chief adviser to the pharaoh. Freud and Jung were not so original when they proposed that dreams were keys to the psyche: they were only transposing an old idea, fraught with mystery and entangled in the world of magic, to a new, more plausible (at least to the modern mind) realm.

Not all dreams, though, are reliable or spiritually potent. This is what makes them so interesting. We never know, so we are forced to trust both the gold and the dross, and to see which, if not both, end up being the most valuable in the end. Try the practice of keeping a pad and pen near your bed, as Myoe did, and writing down your dreams the moment you awaken. You will discover that the difference between the dream and the nondream is not as clear as you might have thought: once you start writing you find yourself adding interesting things to the dream, things that may or may not have actually been in the dream but that seem as if they *ought* to have been. Your dreams improve in the writing of them.

If you keep recording your dreams for a while, you will also discover that there are many kinds of dreams, and each sort brings with it a different valence of feeling. Some dreams seem useless and stupid, catch-all vessels that simply mix up and grind together all sorts of useless details from your waking life, with no particular purpose or form. And then there are dreams that seem clearly important, pure gold, although it is often difficult to know why. The symbols within them seem deep, the emotion full. Sometimes the meanings of these dreams seem completely obvious. Sometimes these obvious meanings are true and useful, and sometimes they are not. But the actual meanings—whatever they may be, and if there are any such meanings—are not translatable into anything other than the dream itself. *The Odyssey* contains many dreams and omens, especially in the last books, when Odysseus, on Ithaca at last, moves toward defeating the suitors and completely possessing his home. Penelope talks to the disguised Odysseus, who thinks he understands one of her dreams. "Ah my friend," seasoned Penelope dissented,

> *dreams are hard to unravel, wayward, drifting things—*
> *not all we glimpse in them will come to pass . . .*
> *Two gates there are for our evanescent dreams,*
> *one is made of ivory, the other made of horn.*
> *Those that pass through the ivory cleanly carved*
> *are will-o'-the-wisps, their message bears no fruit.*
> *The dreams that pass through the gates of polished horn*
> *are fraught with truth, for the dreamer who can see them*[4]

So sleeping and dreaming, and not sleeping and not dreaming, are much more complicated, significant experiences than they seem at first. And Odysseus' coming home to Ithaca at last, not as a conquering hero and not as wily survivor, but as a sleeper carried onto shore by his Phaiakian benefactors is not another case of the failure of awareness or of falling asleep at the wheel. This is not one of Odysseus' mistakes. Instead, we can now appreciate that Odysseus must come home asleep, he must arrive on Ithaca in the arms of his dreams, in a state in which his unconscious mind is given its full due, as it always is in sleep, a state in which we are outside of time, so that all of our lives—past, present, and future—can coexist at once. And this is how we too must return home: we must return with all the experiences we have had in our waking lives throughout the years contained now in a fuller, more mysterious state, a state in which we are more open, more suggestible, and less in control than we would probably like. We all come home asleep.

Some years ago I physically returned home, to the small town in Pennsylvania where I grew up and where I had not lived since I was seventeen. My parents and almost all of my family had been long gone from the place, and I had not visited for decades. I went back then to attend the funeral of a cousin of mine who had died after a long, sad battle with cancer. I was quite close to my cousin, and had felt even closer to her during her slow journey toward death, so when her time came I felt the loss strongly. I flew across the country to the small local airport, rented a car, and drove to the town.

On the way, I stopped at several places that had been important to me in my youth: the house I grew up in, the high school I attended, the Jewish cemetery where many of my relatives were buried. I walked on streets I had walked on every day for years, long ago. I watched the river flow by. I looked up at the dense foliage of the large, old street trees. I felt as if I were in a dream. I thought of my cousin, a vibrant, capable woman, whose voice I would never again hear, whose face I would never again see. Where had she gone? In what way was her absence, now final, different from the absence I had known before, when she was still alive but too far away for me to see her often? Standing in front of the house I grew up in, I wondered, is this house—so sad, so small, and so unfamiliar—really the same house my family had lived in? It was as if life, death, memory, time were all mixed in together, all conspiring to disorient me so that I really couldn't say whether I was "home," or in the most foreign of all possible places.

Perhaps you, too, have felt this and can appreciate how Odysseus must have felt, waking to find himself in a place he could not recognize. In my hometown I felt as if grief and the past had covered everything in a fine mist that made things seem unfamiliar. For Odysseus the mist was physical; the goddess Athena had seen Odysseus asleep and vulnerable and had sprayed a mist all round for his protection. Because the mist made everything look strange and distorted, when Odysseus awoke he was sure that he had not landed on Ithaca at all, and cursed the Phaiakian sailors for their incompetence—or treachery. What sort of place was this? Are the people to be trusted or not? And what about his many treasures? Are they safe or have they already been pilfered by the Phaiakians or some local interlopers? On waking, Odysseus immediately sees to his valuables. While he is doing this, Athena approaches him in the shape of a youthful shepherd. Cunningly, Odysseus ingratiates himself with the youth in order to pump him for information. Overjoyed to learn that, indeed, he is on Ithaca, he nonetheless reflexively spins for Athena a complicated tale about who he is, how he got here, and where he is going. His story amuses the goddess. "You terrible man," she says to him, "foxy, ingenious, never tired of twists and tricks— / so, not even here, on native soil, would you give up / those wily tales that warm the cockles of your heart."[5]

But Odysseus' wiliness is more than habit. Worldly and realistic, a survivor who can afford few illusions and even fewer expectations, he knows he can't simply trust that, after nearly twenty years' absence, he can go bounding up to his home and expect that Penelope, Telemachus, and the rest of the household will be ready to receive him. Chances are good that coming home at last will not signal the end of his travails, that he will have to be cunning and strong, and fight for what is rightfully his. After all, he knows what happened to Agamemnon when *he* returned home after the fighting at Troy: his wife, Clytemnestra, had betrayed him with another man, and no sooner had the great warrior set foot ashore for his triumphal return than he was assassinated by her and her lover.

Athena reveals her identity and lets Odysseus know that many dangers indeed await him, and that his severest trials still lie ahead. He must be willing to endure much more before he is done, and so it is of the utmost importance now that he reveal his true identity to no one—no man, no woman, not a soul. In fact, the careful concealing and the revealing of his identity—at the right time, to the right person, and in the right manner—will occupy Odysseus for the rest of his journey.

It may seem surprising, or quite counterintuitive, that finally arriving home would require us, first of all, to take great care to conceal ourselves. Doesn't coming home mean coming home to our true selves, finally dropping all the masks and standing revealed as we are? Why then is such caution, such deception, necessary?

Perhaps dropping the masks requires that we put them on. This is paradoxical, yet true to life. It's naïve to think that there's a real self behind all the masks, and that when we take off the masks we will find that self. In fact, there's no way not to wear a mask. Our masks are our deceptive, partial, social identities that enable us to operate in the world, to reach out to one another, so that we can be revealed. Wherever we are we've got to be somebody. We always have a role to play. At work we are workers, professionals, managers; in our personal lives we are friends, acquaintances, relatives; at home we are fathers, mothers, spouses, siblings. In the course of any day we put on and take off masks many times. These masks can sometimes make us weary, especially if we feel we have become only a mask. We can long for a freedom beyond our roles, a place of quiet and truth. This is what our hearts have yearned for; this is why we've been journeying all this time toward home.

But once again we've mixed things up, we haven't looked closely enough, we've failed to reckon on the complexity and paradoxical nature of the situation. Just as we have seen that true awareness includes unconsciousness, sleep, and dreams, now we see that fully revealing ourselves requires masks. To think we can throw off the masks and emerge pristinely as "ourselves" is to be like the father who thinks he can be a pal, rather than a dad, to his son. He *can* be a pal, but only by wearing the dad mask. Understanding a mask as a mask, we can wear it properly. Wearing it properly, we can find out what's behind it. A close friend of mine, a Zen priest and business coach, states this succinctly in one of his "business paradoxes." "At work we should be completely ourselves," he writes. "And we must play a role." This wise saying applies to all spheres of life.

What is my mask/role?

18 / Reveal Yourself!

We were compelled to leave home, but going forth taught us that it was necessary to return, and so we began our long, dark, vague voyage back, with our ambivalence, our stuckness, our uncertainty—even about whether there was any journey at all that we needed to take. Finally we opened up enough to begin to face our suffering and the suffering of those around us; we expressed it, encountered mentors on the path, and, encouraged by them, set sail out onto the sea of stories, the exploration of what our lives have been. The quest for homecoming took us through many inevitable disasters in which we suffered a great deal, and our bitter experience taught us that there was no way to pretty up our lives, no way to leave out our darker, more unruly passions as we went forward. Beaten up more than once, we learned humility and endurance. More than once we faltered, but we held on to our commitment and our passion for home, and that sustained us through our many trials and tribulations.

And now, at last, we have arrived on Ithaca, our native land, the place where we began, and to which we have constantly longed to return. It takes us a little while to recognize the place: at first we are suspicious. Even after we do see where we are, we still have reason to be wary, for we know the place is dangerous, that it has not yet been secured. Merely setting foot on native ground again is not enough. There is no magic here that will heal all wounds and

solve all problems immediately. In order for home really to be ours
and to heal us, we must fully possess the place by purifying it of
the suitors, those blind forces of entropy that threaten to destroy
everything. This is arduous work. We know we can't do it alone.

Throughout our journey home we've understandably been
focused on ourselves. We thought coming home meant getting
in touch with ourselves at a deeper level and that that was all
we needed to do. But it is now clear, here on Ithaca, that while
becoming ourselves is essential, it is not sufficient. For this next,
most harrowing part of our ordeal, we will need allies. Before,
we needed only a crew, loyal men who would do our bidding.
Throughout the story, Odysseus' crew is a mere extension of him;
sometimes they stand for his lower instincts, sometimes for his
better self. But the crew are never partners or real friends. At this
point we and Odysseus need loyal loved ones who will stand
shoulder to shoulder with us as, outnumbered, we prepare to fight
the ultimate battle. Now we know that our task involves more
than occupying our true selves; it requires the passion of being
in intimate relationships with others, revealing ourselves fully to
them in love. This last, most moving leg of the journey will force
us to rectify our heartfelt ties to those closest to us. We will have to
reveal ourselves to them so that we can meet them completely.

Not surprisingly, the last books of *The Odyssey* chart the careful, complicated course of Odysseus' revealing his true identity to
those closest to him. Athena, the goddess so adept at deception
that she can see through all mortals' attempts at disguise, is the
first on Ithaca who is privy to who Odysseus really is. She laughs
at Odysseus' false tale, but lets him know that he is right, at this
point, to dissemble, and changes him into a wizened old beggar, a disguise that will enable him to insinuate himself into his
own household without arousing the suitors' suspicions. Beggar-
Odysseus makes his way to the outlying shack of the swineherd
Eumaeus, a simple man who was always loyal to him and who
now kindly takes in the beggar.

At the swineherd's table, Odysseus-in-disguise meets Telemachus, whom Athena has summoned home from his secret journey. Telemachus' quest since Book 1 has been to meet his father, to participate in his power so that he can mature and move forward in his life, but it is impossible for him to see his father as a beggar. Telemachus is polite, but has no inkling who this poor person really is, so Athena changes Odysseus back into a noble warrior, more regal than ever before. Disguised as himself—a great knight in shining armor, character of myth and imagination, the hero of our poem—Odysseus is first recognized by his son.

Telemachus has been searching for his father for so long that he finds it difficult to accept that Odysseus stands before him now, a perfect match for his fantasy. Surely this must be the trick of some god, he thinks. But Odysseus falls on his son with long-deferred emotion, so passionate that Telemachus can't but be convinced, and the two embrace,

> sobbing uncontrollably
> as the deep desire for tears welled up in both.
> They cried out, shrilling cries, pulsing sharper
> than birds of prey—eagles, vultures with hooked claws—
> when farmers plunder their nest of young too young to fly.
> Both men so filled with compassion, eyes streaming tears.[1]

Once they recover from this emotional outburst, they turn to the practical matter at hand: how to defeat the suitors. To the younger man this task seems impossible, for they are overwhelmingly outnumbered. But Odysseus assures his son that, together, and with the gods on their side, they can do it. Odysseus sketches out his plan.

From Odysseus' first significant revelation of identity, we learn that we must begin this phase of our homecoming by expressing the passionate emotion and shrill cries associated with our family lineage. In the Land of the Dead, we've also encountered this profound teaching, when Odysseus met the shade of Anticlea, his mother, and had his first taste of the grief and power of family love. But encountering a living person is much messier than meeting a shade, difficult though that may be. A shade is powerful but a living person is complicated. To meet our living son or father, our mother or daughter demands much more of us, especially when there has been pain, misunderstanding, and disappointment between the two, as there almost always is.

I've seen this dynamic in operation many times with my Zen comrades. One goes a long way in studying the Path, passing many koans, living the monastic life for many years, developing one's character, faith, and understanding. But it almost always happens that a seasoned student must turn back to his or her parents, to understand and forgive them, before his or her path can fully mature. This process is particularly tough when the parent has been an unreliable or destructive force in the practitioner's life—possibly the suffering within the original family is precisely what has caused the practitioner to seek a new family in the Zen lineage. Indeed, initiations in Zen do involve the symbolic leaving of one's native family and the entering into the Buddha's family (in ancient China all monks and nuns legally adopted the Buddha's surname, Shakya). But if this change in lineage is actually to take root, it requires a confrontation with the family of origin and, finally, an acceptance of it. Most moving are the cases in which the practitioner comes to forgive as well as appreciate the damaged, destructive parent, and to feel gratitude for him or her through experiences on the journey home. With the eye of wisdom, the practitioner can see that parents do the best they can, given the powerful conditioning of their circumstances. In any case, thanks to the suffering their many mistakes produced, the life of today has emerged.

Such profound reconciliations can take many years, but they do happen. The practitioner can even come to feel as if his or her own life of truth seeking and precept following functions as a sort of redemption for the destructive life the parent lived: that all the pain of the past has been turned to compassion. Note that *The Odyssey* falls somewhat short of this ideal as Telemachus still idealizes the father: the son is not yet ready to see the beggar-Odysseus; he can only recognize the shining, heroic Odysseus, which is still a disguise. But that's all right. The revelation of children and parents to one another is never perfect; it unfolds over a lifetime.

We can also read the story of the meeting of Odysseus and Telemachus as we would read a dream, in which all the characters represent aspects of ourselves. Looking at it this way, we learn that to produce the force needed to purify and occupy our own house, it's necessary that our youthful, ambivalent, and fearful selves—our Telemachian selves—be united with our wily older selves, because it takes both together to oust the suitors. By himself, Telemachus is stuck. He has no confidence, and knows that if he tries to go forward into battle he will only end up getting in his own way. But neither can Odysseus defeat the suitors on his own, strong and tricky though he may be. He knows this, which is why he's going so slowly and carefully in his plotting instead of storming up to the front door of his house, as he'd like to. The wisdom and craft of age needs the innocence and desire of youth to be effective. This means that as we grow older we must make a new pact with our youth, our passion, our idealism, and our need to search and question, because if we abandon all that, age's weight will wear us down. The Odysseus in us must reveal himself to the Telemachus in us, so that together they have the strength to prevail. Until life's last breath, we have work to do, things to discover and marvel over, even in the very process of aging and dying—as we will see later.

From here on, the final books of *The Odyssey* chart the complex, nuanced course of Odysseus' further insights, as he struggles to clarify the most important relationships of his lifetime in preparation for the final assault on the suitors. The exciting plot ends with two bloody battles and a mass execution, but behind this violent extravaganza is the subtle dance Odysseus dances within himself and with his loved ones, as he prepares to truly meet them.

Oddly, the next creature to discover Odysseus' true identity is not his devastated wife or his grieving father, but Argos, his old dog. Although the human beings closest to Odysseus are unable to pierce through his beggar's disguise to see the true person, as soon as the exhausted, tick-infested Argos, lying on a dungheap, sees the old beggar approaching, he rouses himself. He knows his master and tries to run to him. But the excitement is too much for the old beast, and he dies on the spot. At first this may seem a dismaying portent: the most loyal and true of Odysseus' supporters dies at first sight of him. But this sad moment also has another side we must take soberly to heart: our most comfortable and comforting identities must die before we can find our true place at home.

Later, Eurycleia, Penelope's old servant and Odysseus' childhood maid, discovers the truth about the beggar's identity as she bathes his tired feet, seeing on his leg the scar that Odysseus received as a youth, when he was gored by a wild boar while hunting at his grandfather's house. The scar is unmistakable and Odysseus has no choice now but to say who he is. He swears Eurycleia to secrecy, for the time is not yet right for Penelope or anyone else to know his true identity.

Still later, as the time for battle draws near, Odysseus reveals himself to Eumaeus, the swineherd, and Philoetius, the cowherd, knowing that these simple, loyal retainers will accept him immediately and will fight with him side by side. When the battle finally begins, Odysseus also reveals himself to the suitors, who are aghast to know that the man they've assumed dead has finally come to kill them all.

All these revelations are fairly straightforward and practical, but for the most important remaining people to whom Odysseus must fully reveal himself—Penelope, his wife, and Laertes, his father—the process is fraught with difficulty. As in life so in *The Odyssey*—the most intimate, most salient relationships take a good deal of doing to get right.

A further word about that identifying scar on Odysseus' leg,

which becomes a crucial detail as the story unfolds: Odysseus'
grandfather, Autolycus (the name means "the wolf himself"), was
a well-known thief and liar. It was he who named Odysseus, and
at this point in the story we learn the meaning of our hero's name:
Odysseus means "Son of Pain." Odysseus' identifying scar *is* his
name, the indelible mark of who he is: his pain can't be hidden,
for it is a mark on his body.

How we wish we could hide our pain—from ourselves if possible, but if not from ourselves, at least from others. It's so embar-
rassing to be as vulnerable as we are, as messed up inside as we
so often find ourselves. So we learn to dissemble quite effectively,
just as Odysseus does; it seems absolutely necessary to do so. We
develop convincing personae and clever strategies to cover up
our wounds, which can work well. Many people function quite
nicely at work, and sometimes even in their personal lives, while
inside their pain is so great that they can't ever acknowledge it
and so hold at arm's length the inner disappointment, sorrow, and
fear. But this effort is not without cost. Sometimes it makes us ill.
Sometimes it merely makes us unhappy. Almost always it isolates
us. When we hold up a happy face to the world we are met by
other happy faces, which is pleasant enough, but we know that
these smooth meetings are not true meetings, so they leave us
unsatisfied and lonely: we feel as unmet as we actually are.

Only when we are willing and able to show ourselves, revealing our scars and scrapes from the past, as Odysseus here can't
help but do, can we really meet and be met by one another. Then
we realize that our scars were visible all along and that our deepest pain has been our truest name. Still, it takes courage to cut
through our embarrassment and pride and admit to others that we
suffer. When we do, we find that they have the same scars we do.
It's a tremendous relief to recognize that others have suffered just
as we have, and that our problems are not just our problems, they
are *the* problems, human problems.

Another of my many Zen friends has recently been diagnosed
with amyotrophic lateral sclerosis (ALS), a totally debilitating ill-

ness that is almost always fatal, usually in a matter of only a few years. He told me that after the diagnosis he and his wife did a lot of crying. Then came the depression. What, he asked himself, was the point of going on, when going on was going to mean the loss of all his faculties, and his eventual death? And how could this happen to him, and why? The depression was severe enough that he sought medical help and was put on antidepressant drugs, which seemed to work. After a time, he told me, he was able to see one great advantage in his condition: it brought him closer to people. When he told his friends one by one about it, he noticed that the tenor of the conversation changed. From then on, the relationships became more intimate and emotionally satisfying. Hearing his honest, unashamed explanation of his troubles, his friends opened up and began to share their troubles, too. Many of his friends—far more than he'd ever imagined—told him that they too suffered from depression and had for some time; they even used the same antidepressants that he was taking. This astonished my friend, who had had no idea that depression was so common, or that people he'd known and been close to for many years had been suffering from it. Far from his illness isolating him in his private pain, he was now connected to many others who were emboldened to open up to their "scars" by the way he'd taken on what was happening to him. Now, he told me, every time he picked up the phone or answered the door there was the possibility that he was in for an intense, emotional encounter. These encounters weren't necessarily joyful, but they were, he said, always happy, for even when he ended up in tears, with his interlocutor also in tears, they were good tears, tears of connection and commiseration. These days of his illness were precious days, in some ways more precious than any he'd ever known.

Please take a moment to consider this personally. Think of some pain that has come to you in your life, an illness, a loss, a rejection, betrayal, or disappointment. How did you feel (or how do you feel, if you are considering a present condition)? That something that ought not to have happened had happened? That it was someone else's fault? That it was your fault? That it was God's fault or the world's fault? Did you feel alone, diminished, a person less than others? Were you frightened?

Now think, "That was not my pain, it was *the* pain. Whatever I have felt, whatever I have suffered, others have also felt, also suffered. In suffering this I am understanding them. In suffering this my heart connects to theirs."

How do you feel now?

Think now of the world's suffering. Of the anguish of the many people involved in violent struggle, whether in far-off wars or in their own homes. Of the pain of those who are ill, alone, oppressed, hungry. And think, "This pain is not their pain. It is *the* pain, human pain. I need not feel distant from these people. I need not pity them. In feeling my own pain I feel theirs; in feeling their pain I feel my own."

Can you find some calmness in this recognition?

Human pain, whether emotional, spiritual, or physical, is never "my" pain or "their" pain, it is always "the" pain. When we realize this our pain is not so painful. As my friend with ALS discovered, a kind of beauty and profound connection with others can come when we are willing to meet one another in the midst of our shared human vulnerability.

19 / Love's Risk

For some years now I have been rereading and rethinking Martin Buber's great book *I and Thou*, which sets forth the "you and it" philosophy I referred to earlier. The book's thesis is echoed in the teachings of Mahayana Buddhism, which holds that there is no "I" apart from our connection to another.

When we were infants we knew this. We innocently loved everything, incorporating everything into ourselves. But we soon learned we couldn't keep this up. We got feedback from the world that our wishes and needs were not the only things that mattered. In fact, they mattered very little. This was shocking. It hurt and disappointed us, and this hurt and disappointment became our education: we learned that we have to be tough and clever, Odysseus-like, if we are to get what we want and need. Like our hero, we went forth to Troy to make our name in battle and preserve our honor. We grew up and learned how to survive in this hostile world; we became someone, made our name, took our place. We made our way in the world as wily, wary, isolated individuals.

But we eventually found this alienating and exhausting. Dealing with the world every day takes its toll; it is stressful. As Odysseus found in the ordeal of the Cyclops, sometimes to save ourselves we need to appreciate that we also have to be Nobody, even though we have worked very hard to be Somebody. Disappearing from the world is a necessity sometimes.

Buber, like Mahayana Buddhism, proposes something even further. Beyond Somebody (the harsh world over against us) and Nobody (the world dissolved) is the world as lover and friend. When we arrive home at last on Ithaca, we are by necessity called on to enact this possibility. This is the task with which we complete our journey. Through revealing ourselves fully to those we love, we come to recognize that we have never really been separate Somebodies; we have always been brought to life in relationship to someone else or with someone else. This has been so every moment of our lives. We are not so much persons as ever-shifting points of meeting. We have always created and been created by those with whom we've shared our lives. In Mahayana Buddhism this essential teaching about the always-connected nature of the self is emphasized as compassion: the path of love is not one option among many, it is the only path there is, for it is embedded in our very nature as persons. All religions teach this. And now that we've arrived at last on Ithaca, it's time for us to test this out, to risk ourselves in love, as Odysseus now must do.

Buber's philosophy of dialogue helps us understand how to do this. Inspired by the biblical imagery of his Jewish heritage, in which God speaks the world into being, Buber sees life's encounters as opportunities for us to open up our mouths and express ourselves. For Buber, life is a speaking, a telling, a story. Life is engagement in dialogue. As we've been saying all along, to undertake our life's homecoming journey is to sail out onto the sea of stories; there we must accept our story and share it with others. It is necessary that we speak our life, that someone listen to us, and that we listen to another person. Even when we are not speaking, our mere appearance in this world is a kind of speech, for by simply being who we are and appearing as we do we express our lives. Receiving the presence of another is receiving that person's word.

Buber speaks of the two sorts of words we can utter, I-it or I-you. Buber's famous hyphen is telling and very skillful. It makes two words into one, yet at the same time they remain two. I-it or I-you doesn't mean that I and It or I and You merge into a one-word oneness. With merging there is no relationship, no dialogue, no mutual responsibility; there is only the oneness into which we both dissolve; *Iit* and *Iyou* are not intelligible words. I-you or I-it is not dissolving, but relationship, engagement, connection. There can be no me without a you or an it. There can be no person without another. Even when I am alone I am in relation: to sky, air, memory, language, thought—and therefore to others. The human being who exists without others is impossible.

Though we must live in both I-it and I-you there is a crucial difference between them. Buber expresses it like this: "The basic word I-you can only be spoken with one's whole being. The basic word I-it can never be spoken with one's whole being. . . . Whoever says you does not have something; he has nothing. But he stands in relation."[1]

This notion had large existential and religious implications in Buber's life and thought. The story goes that Buber developed his I-you philosophy after an encounter he had early in his academic career. He was approached one day in his study by a disturbed student who wanted to discuss his personal problems with the already esteemed professor Buber. Not wanting to be impolite, but still preoccupied with his studies, Buber heard the young man out, but without giving him much attention. Later that day the man committed suicide, and for the rest of his life Buber remained convinced that had he only listened and met the man more fully he would have saved his life. This is why Buber regarded the practice of meeting the other completely and sympathetically as the primary practice in living, and the primary fact of life.

I hear, too, in Buber's thought echoes of one of the most important teachings of my own Soto Zen lineage, the teaching of face-to-face transmission. The training of a contemporary Soto Zen priest, unlike that of rabbis, ministers, or Catholic priests, is an apprenticeship: there are no seminaries from which Soto Zen priests are graduated. Instead, the basic training involves a face-to-face relationship with a mentoring priest. Student and teacher practice side by side in retreat or monastic training periods, living together for short or long periods of time, absorbing the flavor of each other's being until enough time has gone by that they have in some real sense mixed and merged together, but in a "hyphenated" way, that is, without either of them losing his or her autonomy and personal pungency.

After long years practicing together in this way and going through various life changes and crises, a ceremony of face-to-face transmission occurs. This private, fairly elaborate ceremony has always seemed to me to be a ritualized enactment of precisely what Buber is suggesting in his I-you philosophy. In Buberian terms, when you receive face-to-face transmission from your teacher in the Soto Zen ceremony you have nothing, but you stand in relation. The hope is that, whether or not the newly transmitted priest knows much about Zen doctrine or has had profound meditation experiences, he or she is well grounded in the life that flows from the teachings, and is willing and able now to stand in relation to the teacher as well as everyone and everything.

This face-to-face meeting is of course not limited to formal Zen priest practice. Every day of our lives we are presented with opportunities for meeting in an I-you way; every encounter with another person is a new chance to let go of our normal paranoia and take the risk of stepping, unprotected, into the life of another, and to let that other step into our life. We are invited, over and over again, to speak our word, tell our story, and to listen.

Take a moment now to practice this teaching. Sit comfortably, breathing in and out with awareness. Settle yourself gently, allowing whatever wants to come to mind or heart. Now begin to listen to sounds inside the room and out. Remain in touch with your body and breath as you do this; being with the body and breath will help you to listen more acutely. Imagine that you are listening not only with your ears but with your whole body, so that the sound penetrates you right through.

Notice that at first you only hear a little. But as you continue to listen, more and more sound becomes available to you. It is surprising how much sound you had not heard until you actually tried to listen.

Notice how each sound immediately evokes its identifying words and concomitant thoughts: "That's a car going by outside, a little too fast; there's the refrigerator's hum, doesn't sound right; the clock's tick, so quiet, wonder what time it is." Notice that all this removes you slightly from the sound, as if the sound's identifying label and accompanying thoughts painted themselves as a subtle coating on top of the sound, muffling it, distancing it from you.

Let yourself be more quiet. See if you can gently let go of identifying labels and thoughts and simply meet each sound, be met by each sound. Let the sounds be soft and softly enter you.

Sit this way for as long as you like, simply listening to sound, without identifying it, without trying to change it, just taking it in, fully and intimately.

Imagine listening to another person this way: without labeling the person as someone, without evaluating or naming what you are hearing, without jumping immediately to respond.

Next time you have a chance, listen this way to someone.

Imagine someone listening to you in this way.

I present all this in order to take you more deeply into what Odysseus is now experiencing as he prepares to meet his loved ones face-to-face in the next, most crucial step in his journey. But at this point it makes less sense to speak about a journey since we have arrived on Ithaca and have nowhere further we need to go.

From here on there will be no more getting lost at sea, no more monsters and sorceresses, no more hair-raising trials and narrow escapes. Having been through the necessary disasters and struggles, you are where you need to be. The challenge now is not to journey on but rather to stay firmly where you are with courage and strength. The suitors must be defeated and this will entail a bloody battle. And that battle can only be fought after the most important I-you meetings of your life have taken place.

Let's return to our tale:

Penelope summons the beggar-Odysseus, for she has heard that the old man has news of her husband. She asks him who he is and where he is from, but the beggar refuses to say: it is too painful to recall, he tells her. But at Penelope's urging he finally tells his tale—that he is a king's son from Crete who's fallen on hard times, that he knew Odysseus years ago, and once hosted him in his palace—and the tale is quite convincingly full of detail and color, for Odysseus "knows how to say many false things that are like true sayings."[2] But Penelope is suspicious. This is not the first time someone has claimed knowledge of her husband. To test the beggar she asks him what Odysseus wore all those years ago when they met, and of course the beggar passes the test. He tells her more: that Odysseus is alive, he's being brought to Ithaca by the Phaiakians, he'll soon return to do in the suitors. This Penelope can't let herself believe, for she wants it too badly: no, this is not possible, she says. Surely my husband is dead. On this note the reunion so long hoped and suffered for ends. Face-to-face for the first time in twenty years, the couple part company for the night as strangers. They do not meet again until after the suitors have been slain, when Odysseus is restored to his own appearance. Even then—after all the wanderings, captivity, shipwrecks, and battles, when he is more than ready to take his wife into his arms, and he expects that she feels the same—Penelope is still wary. One can't depend on looks or even the sound of a voice, as the gods can be tricky and cruel to those who allow themselves to be taken in. "You are so strange," he tells her, exasperated. "The gods have made your heart more stubborn than the rest of womankind." "*You* are so strange," she says in return.[3] To test her husband once more, she pretends to order the servants to drag the bed out of their bedroom so that Odysseus—if it is Odysseus!—can sleep alone. Irritated, he tells her that she ought to know that the bed can't be moved, because it is anchored to an olive tree: no man, however strong, could hope to move it. Only Odysseus could know this, and so, at last, Penelope accepts him. Athena suspends the dawn's usual arrival time so that husband and wife can enjoy each other for a sweet, lengthened night, during which they "reveled in all / the longed-for joys of love, reveled in each other's stories"[4]—this time without deception.

This strangely elaborate courtship drags on over several books of *The Odyssey* and shows us that meeting the beloved is not as simple and straightforward as we hope. Though we may feel open and ready for the encounter, we find that there are complications and contradictions within and between us we didn't know were there. We may recognize one another, but at the same time we may not. We may be more wary of one another than we know. It's not so easy to give ourselves in love, especially the sort of love that Odysseus and Penelope have, which involves many years of knowing one another but also many years of absence, of not knowing one another. This not knowing makes it difficult to trust love and difficult to trust the other, for we've been scarred, and we need to protect ourselves.

When we come to the point in our journey when it is absolutely necessary that we meet, we must do so by speaking our words, telling our tales. But we have been through so much by now that it is impossible for us to fool ourselves any longer. We are skeptics, aware of the essential deception that lies at the heart of every story. But we can't help it. As we learned earlier when we spoke about false stories, we need false tales, if only to advance the plot; no stories are absolutely true. So we must meet with some deception, there's no getting around it. But this creates a risk. Knowing neither ourselves nor another perfectly, how can we be sure we won't be betrayed? How do we know we won't end up sooner or later, as so many do, devastated when we recognize suddenly that the life we thought we'd been living, the love we thought we'd enjoyed, was simply an illusion? I have seen too much of this in marriages and partnerships of all sorts to believe that anyone is immune to it. "How strange you are!" is a sentence any one of us might utter to any other of us at any time, and although we might utter it in appreciation and wonder, we might also utter it with trepidation. How much do we know anyone, and how much can we really count on anyone? No wonder it is hard to reveal ourselves, hard to trust, difficult to love. No wonder Penelope is so reluctant to accept Odysseus.

Let's take a moment to practice with this disturbing reality.

First, imagine your life as it stretches back toward the past. See its shape. Feel its texture. If it has a color, see the color. If it has a sound, listen to the sound. Think of all the changes that have occurred in your life, all the different people you have been. Recall yourself as a child, an adolescent, a young adult, an older person. Each so different from the other. Remember things you have done or said that surprised you, things you are proud of now, things you are ashamed of. Realize that you are now and have always been in the process of becoming yourself. That as much as you know yourself, this knowledge is necessarily imperfect and constantly subject to revision.

Now think of the people in your life. If you know yourself imperfectly, your knowledge of them must be even more sketchy. At least you know yourself from the inside. You can understand your own intentions and motivations to some extent. But others, even those most intimate to you, can only be known by their actions and words. You cannot know their intentions, their inmost feelings, their hopes and fears.

Take a few moments to breathe this fact into your heart. Think how much faith, how much trust, it takes to accept and love another person fully. Breathe with that faith, that trust.

In the dance of Odysseus and Penelope's meeting we can sense an important underlying issue: fear. We've met this obstacle before. In the Land of the Dead, Odysseus was "green with fear," paralyzed with terror, but that was the sort of spine-chilling, horror-movie fear we know about, the fear of darkness, death, noises in the night, creepy fear that titillates and passes, as it did eventually for Odysseus. But there is another sort of fear that is far worse than this, because it is so pervasive and so basic that it may be within us most of the time, even when we don't know it.

I am impressed with the pervasiveness of fear. I talk to many people about their spiritual lives and very often the question of fear arises. People who function quite well and live successful lives, even successful personal lives, tell me that deep down they are quite afraid. Of what? Of life, of death, of failure. They are afraid of engaging their lives fully without holding back because they are afraid that if they don't hold something in reserve they might end up with nothing. They are afraid of loving wholeheartedly for fear they will be rejected, and they are afraid that if they don't love wholeheartedly they'll never be able to love. And they are afraid that they will never be really loved, and if they are loved, they are afraid that they are unworthy of that love and so are sure to lose it. Maybe all of this is ridiculous and these people are manufacturing problems where none exist. But their fear is quite real to them and it makes a tremendous difference in the way they feel and live their lives.

Years ago some Zen practitioners and I spent a month studying anger. We studied traditional Buddhist teachings about anger, which take two forms: awareness of body, breath, and thought as anger arises; and the intentional cultivation of antidotes that we can apply, such as loving kindness or generosity. As we tried out these practices, and observed our daily lives, to see what we could discover, we found that anger and irritation, which we took to be a mild form of anger, are shockingly common, and arise many times a day.

On close examination we saw that most of the time anger is a mask for fear. We don't want to feel fear, which is disempowering and uncomfortable, so we get angry instead. But what are we afraid of? Things don't go as we would like them to; the world is not cooperative with our wishes and needs. There is nothing we can do about this. This is a frightening fact. Furthermore, we know that we are vulnerable, subject on a daily basis to unwanted change and finally to death. Our situation is fundamentally shaky and this is terrifying—so instead of facing all this we get angry or irritated about this or that that has gone wrong. Fear is deep and fundamental, more than an emotion among many other emotions.

What is anger? It is the powerful urge to harm. This distinguishes toxic anger from what we might call "righteous anger," which is a motivation to right injustice rather than to harm. The most important aspect of reflection on anger is to recognize its harmful nature; anger is destructive to self and others; anger never heals. Since we are all victims of anger, we need to be forgiving of the anger of others, as well as our own. Just as kindling and spark produce fire, so anger arises when conditions for it are present. When anger flares it is not your fault, but it is your responsibility to reduce the flames and not to fan them. The Zen precept is not "do not be angry." It is "do not *harbor* anger." Do not fan it or add more fuel.

We can practice mindfulness of anger by recognizing anger as it is and committing to overcome it little by little. When anger arises, know "This is anger, this is how it feels, in the body, in the heart, in the mind." As much as possible try simply to be aware of the concrete unpleasant experience of anger without moving from it to blame and then to speak or act angrily. This disconnecting from the habit of reacting angrily and instead observing your anger takes patience, craft, and time. But it is possible.

Additionally, you might work to cultivate antidotal emotions. In your regular meditation practice, you can develop feelings of loving kindness toward individuals or toward people in general. You can do this through repetition of phrases such as "May so-and-so, and may all beings be happy, may they be content, and may causes of misery be removed from them." You can begin by wishing for such benefit for yourself, then others. In this way you will be predisposing your heart to kindness, so that when conditions for anger arise within you some kindness will already be there, softening your heart as it begins to harden. Then, at the time you begin to be angry you can practice these phrases of loving kindness and compassion and disconnect yourself from an angry response.

In these ways, and others that you can study or invent yourself, you can cultivate your emotional state more and more in the direction of patience and love, rather than hotheadedness and hardheartedness. The more you are willing to admit and investigate your anger, the more you will see the fear that is behind it. When you are willing to see and hold your fear, your anger becomes more manageable.

The *New Yorker*'s drama critic John Lahr once wrote an astonishing piece for the magazine, "Petrified: The Horrors of Stage Fright." Stage fright is common and debilitating, even to seasoned performers. We imagine that stars like Laurence Olivier, Carly Simon, and Barbra Streisand overcame whatever fears they may have had of going onstage early in their careers, or else how could they possibly function? But it's not so. Their stories are told in the article; each of them suffered from severe panic every time they performed, throughout their careers, and all had to find ways to cope with it. In his sixties, Olivier contemplated leaving the stage because of it. The pianist Glenn Gould was so terrified of performing that he stopped doing it. The article begins with the spectacular case of British writer-actor Stephen Fry, whose stage fright came on suddenly one day with such severity that after an abortive suicide attempt he left the country without notice in the middle of the run of a play he was starring in. His mysterious disappearance was written about in the English papers for months.

The Buddha himself seemed to appreciate that people are terrified by standing up in front of an audience even to do something that they are quite skilled at, and very much loved for. In Buddhism, among the fearful things discussed are fear of death, fear of loss of reputation, and fear of public speaking. There is something inherently terrifying about revealing ourselves to others. Though we are seen by others every day, and though as performers we are in some sense shielded from the audience by the role we are playing, somehow the experience of getting up in front of others to perform evokes an archetypal terror. We fear that we will stand there nakedly revealed as we really are, seen *through,* as it were, and found to be fundamentally inadequate, or even somehow nonexistent. We fear we won't survive the scrutiny.

Odysseus goes beyond this fear. He is finally able to stand revealed before Penelope as he truly is, and so can connect with everything in his life, with her, with his own emotion, with the rest of his family, and with everyone else. At last he turns his restless trickiness into love, his long and troubled exile into home.

There is something wonderful about the fact that the penultimate moment on Odysseus' journey home is not a battle, a spiritual insight, or a political victory, but a domestic reconciliation. This is true to life. The accomplishment of outward or even inward achievement is neither as difficult nor as rewarding as the ripening of love. It's easy enough to establish a career and to get better and better at what you do: it takes effort and diligence, but as time goes by it gets easier, and the rewards, both material and psychological, increase. It's also not so hard to develop a certain degree of self-knowledge or spiritual wisdom; we can seek help, read books, attend meetings or services, and gradually gain confidence. Nor is it difficult to begin an intimate personal relationship: one's inner desires and dreams propel you forward and things seem to happen as if by themselves.

But it is much tougher to sustain an intimate relationship with real heart over many years. The only way to do this is to be willing to be surprised and confused, sometimes frustrated and dissatisfied: not try to understand or fix all the time, but to allow the very confusion and frustration to carry you beyond them. You necessarily reinvent your intimate relationships over and over again and every time you do you feel uncertainty and some discomfort. As time goes on, we naturally weary of one another; we think we know who the other is and what to expect. We define and inure ourselves to supposed character quirks and problems, and in this way shut down the possibility of refreshed love. Most people I know struggle with their marriages and partnerships. Even when things are going fine they are not necessarily easy or smooth. But those few who manage to see that in their intimate relationships lie life's most difficult, most rewarding, challenges, feel a growing sense of wonder and appreciation as time goes by, as well as gratitude for the unlikely miracle of lasting love in the messy human world. To create a relationship that is truly loving in a world so full of hatred and confusion is an achievement of the first rank, one that we all recognize and celebrate when we see it.

In classical Zen and Buddhist practice, which is based on a monastic model, there is no lore about intimate relationships. In leaving his family behind to begin his spiritual quest, the Buddha was saying, in effect, "Family love is too difficult; give it up if you want to be enlightened!" Instead of emphasizing love for one person, or a few people, Buddhism and Zen encourage the practice of universal compassion, certainly a laudable ideal. In Zen we even take the vow, "Sentient beings are numberless; I vow to save them." But it may be easier to practice this idealistic virtue of universal compassion, to love "all sentient beings," than it is to love one actual person. It may be easier to "save" all than actually to take care of one person who lives in your house. But if you can take care of that one person, you will be practicing realistic rather than idealistic compassion, the next necessary step on the journey home. This is why Odysseus' reconciliation with Penelope comes at this juncture in our story. How could we come home without love?

When earlier we spoke of developing loving kindness as an antidote to anger, we worked with the phrases "May all beings be happy, may they be content, and may causes of misery be removed from them." Now, practice these phrases and specifically include your partner, spouse, or most cherished loved one. Think of your loved one, see her smiling before you. "May she be happy; may her heart be open; may she find contentment and peace." By practicing this every day, you will help to keep alive within you the preciousness of this person to you, and to refresh and strengthen your positive wishes for her.

Ultimately, universal love and compassion—and love and compassion for one person—depend on each other. What sort of universal love would we have if we couldn't love one person as he or she actually is? And what sort of love of one person would we be feeling if that love were selfish and exclusive, depending on that one person to fulfill our needs, or loving that one person and being indifferent to others? When you are in love, you love everyone and everything, for this is what the beloved inspires. Though it may not be obvious at first and may take a lifetime to understand truly, love can never be selfish or exclusive. Selfish, exclusive love is possessive; it easily turns to hatred. Real love can't be possessive. To love your spouse or partner unselfishly, and to make that unselfish love real on a day-to-day basis, is one of the best ways I know to train in the Zen vow to save all sentient beings. Since beings are numberless, saving them all is not a matter of saving more and more of them. There's no end to that. In loving each one we love all. Through the love of one comes the love of many. Earlier, when we spoke about finding an inspiring vision we quoted the verse of Santideva:

And as long as space endures,
As long as there are beings to be found,
May I continue likewise to remain
To drive away the sorrows of the world.

This is the spirit of true homecoming. Love is the highest of all achievements, the best of all protections. This is why now, as we approach the end of our story, it is love that holds sway, love that is honored and strengthened.

In Greece, the olive is sacred and foundational. Odysseus and Penelope established their home around an olive tree, built their bed and therefore their house around it. And the olive tree brought them together after so many years. Their love is rooted in earth, in the sacred outer world that serves as the center of their home. Romantic love has no such roots. It is founded on passion—and on pain, because there is no passion without pain. Romantic lovers merge. In merging, as we learn from Buber, each of them passes away and so does the world. There is no hyphen between them, and that's a condition that can't last for long. The revealed love that Odysseus and Penelope now know is an I-you love, established after long struggle. Although Odysseus and Penelope can't live forever, the love they share is larger than they are, infinite, expandable, and all-inclusive.

There is more to the olive tree. It is Athena's tree, her gift to the people of Athens, who repaid her by naming their city in her honor. Athena is called the "gray-eyed one." Olive leaves are gray underneath, and when the wind turns them over they flash the goddess' striking eyes. Like all trees, the olive is strong, steady, steadfast.

The word *tree* comes from the same root word as the word

trust, as well as *truce* and *pledge.* To me the actual physical presence of trees is the very embodiment of trust, solidity, faithfulness, and dignity. Trees are great spiritual teachers and I sometimes recommend that people study Zen with a tree, that they stand under or next to a tree for a while, or walk quietly and mindfully among trees. The term *tree hugger* has become a jokey, pejorative term, but one could do worse than be a tree hugger. If you try to hug a tree, paying close attention while you are doing it, you will find it a powerful experience.

When I first began practicing Zen years ago, I lived alone in the middle of a redwood forest. Every day I would go out and sit under a redwood tree and, with my back to the tree, look up the trunk and past the canopy to the circle of sky beyond. In a completely different way I have been moved by white pines, small gnarled trees I have seen growing at timberline in the High Sierra. These noble creatures endure hardships and thrive. They, too, have quite a presence.

Trees figure prominently in the story of the Buddha. His mother gave birth to him while leaning against a tree. On the night of his enlightenment he sat under a tree. And he died lying on the earth between two trees. Trees are strong physical presences as well as metaphors for aspects of the inner life.

Being a Zen veteran, I can't hear the word *tree* without thinking of my favorite Zen Master, Zhaozho, and his famous dialogue:

Monk: What is the meaning of Bodhidharma's coming
     from the West?
Zhaozho: The cypress tree in the courtyard.
Monk: Teacher, please don't teach me about outside
     things; I am asking about inner truth.
Zhaozho: I'm not teaching you about outside things.
Monk: Then what is the meaning of Bodhidharma's coming from the West?
Zhaozho: The cypress tree in the courtyard.

In Zen, the question "Why did Bodhidharma come from the West?" is the question, "What is the deepest meaning of the Teachings, of our human life?" Zhaozho's answer points to what's most essential and most profound about our experience of meeting. When we meet another—whether that other is a person or an oak tree, but especially if it's a person—everything is there, the whole of the truth. If we say it's an "inner" experience, that's not quite right. Nor are we meeting something "outside" ourselves. Meeting is neither inside nor outside, it is I-you, inside and outside hyphenated. Zhaozho's deceptively simple words express the Zen version of what Odysseus and Penelope have learned now that their long years of presence and absence, loyalty and longing, have finally culminated in their truly meeting one another. When we find the courage to meet intimately, we support and are supported by the whole world.

20 / On the Threshold

I n order to analyze the meeting between Odysseus and Penelope, I had to telescope it. Between their first conversation and their eventual reconciliation comes the climactic moment of our story: the bloody battle in which Odysseus, Telemachus, the swineherd Eumaeus, and the cowherd Philoetius finally defeat and kill the suitors. This is where our tale has been taking us all along, because *The Odyssey* is a tale of adventure in which a battle would certainly seem to be the culminating event. But stirring as it may be, the defeat of the suitors is much more than a heroic military victory, and it is not the resolution of the story: the resolution is the meeting that we have been talking about; the battle is its necessary precondition. Odysseus must accomplish this final, necessary victory over himself before he can reconcile and completely embrace Penelope, love, and home.

The battle's catalyst is, in fact, Penelope, for, despite her great reluctance, she feels she can no longer put off the suitors. The ploy that worked for three years—the weaving by day and unweaving by night of the shroud she'd been making for her grieving father-in-law, Laertes—who all assumed would soon die—has been discovered. She feels she can't allow Telemachus to continue forever stuck in a life on hold. And she's feeling pressure from her parents to give up hope of Odysseus' return and move on with her life. Since she cannot bring herself to choose one of the suitors, she devises a contest. She'll take Odysseus' bow out of the storeroom. Whichever of the suitors can string the bow and shoot through a line of ax handles planted in the ground will be her next husband.

The day of the contest arrives. Odysseus attends, still in his disguise as a beggar. To rouse Odysseus' pride and wrath, Athena whips up the suitors' scorn of the beggar and they insult and revile him even worse than before. Telemachus astounds them by dressing them down with strong words. When they remark on this change that has come over him he tells them, "The boy you knew is gone." When the contest begins, several of the suitors try to string the bow but none can do it, even after softening it with oil and heat from the fire. With each failure, their embarrassment mounts: it's bad enough not to be the one to win the prize of Penelope's hand, but even worse to be known as a weakling in comparison with Odysseus, who could string that bow with ease. Joking nervously, the suitors decide to put the contest off for a while: back to eating and drinking till another day.

Penelope watches all this as she "leans against a pillar that sustains the roof," the position she always takes when she observes the suitors, an appropriate spot for the woman whose intense loyalty and emotional endurance serve as the bulwark of our tale. Yet she is sent away and does not witness the next events. Beggar-Odysseus is stationed in *his* spot on the threshold of the entrance to the great hall, where he has been during all the days he's been coming to the palace. He offers to try the bow. The suitors resist, horrified at even the remote possibility that the beggar would show them up, but Telemachus, with his newfound nerve, insists, and has his way. To their shock, Odysseus strings the bow, shoots through the axes, and defiantly shouts out his identity, "Curs! Little did you imagine I'd return from Troy! Now you'll pay the price for what you've done."[1] The battle is on.

Telemachus, Odysseus, and the two loyal husbandmen fight standing shoulder to shoulder on the threshold. Odysseus shoots all his arrows, and each shaft finds its mark. Suitors topple onto the banquet tables; food, wine, weapons, splattered blood, and heavy furniture fly across the room. Arrows gone, the heroes take up spear, sword, and shield, and the battle continues until all the suitors are slain. They "lay in heaps, corpse covering corpse," all 108 of them. (Curiously, 108 is the number of beads on Buddhist and Hindu rosaries; in Buddhism 108 stands for the totality of human delusions to be overcome by practice.) Swiftly, Odysseus moves to purify his household: the maidservants who have betrayed Penelope, acting as spies and consorts for the suitors, are brutally executed; sulfur and fire are brought to fumigate the palace rooms, and now the loyal serving women, who have been hidden away,

> *came crowding out of their quarters, torch in hand,*
> *flung their arms around Odysseus, hugged him, home at last,*
> *and kissed his head and shoulders, seized his hands, and he,*
> *overcome by a lovely longing, broke down and wept.*[2]

It is noteworthy that Odysseus and his tiny band of helpers stand on the threshold of his house as they fight off the suitors. Like a tree, a threshold is a suggestive image: it is the liminal place, the in-between place; it is neither inside nor outside, and is both entrance and exit. It is strategically important for Odysseus and his small band to stand on the threshold where they can block the suitors' escape. The threshold is thus a powerful, pivotal, essential location. Like now, the time where life begins and ends, and here, the place from which we move forward or back, the threshold is the balance point, the origin as well as the ending point. It is where we, like Odysseus and his loyal band of heroes, must take our stand.

The journey home, as we've been saying, is life's journey, time's journey, the spiritual journey. Now, at this nearly final stage of the journey, we find ourselves standing at the threshold. The word comes from *thresh* (*thrash* is the same word), which means to beat or pound, as in threshing grain or thrashing out an agreement.

One form of threshing or thrashing is treading, stomping, hence *threshold,* the stone or board at the entrance to the house on which you must tread in order to go from outside to inside or inside to outside. When you are on the threshold you are poised to go in or out. You are, as we say, on the threshold of something.

And so it is for us at this moment of our journey. We stand at the threshold as beggars, beat-up old fools, pounded, thrashed, and made ragged by all we have been through, but at the same time still wily enough and strong enough to fight this last crucial battle, and perhaps more ready for it precisely because of all we've been through. The threshold divides not only the inside from the outside of the house, it also divides the outer life that has occupied us for so long from the inner life toward which we have been moving more and more. We are on the threshold that divides the relative youth that has been ours till now from the old age to which we are going. And, yes, we are also on the threshold that divides the life that is all we have ever known from the inconceivable death we are approaching.

As we've said, the suitors are entropy, inertia, inner profligacy, the tendency in each of us toward weakness and the gradual dissipation of our spirit as life goes on. It's simply hard to keep our energy and enthusiasm going as we get older, having seen more and more in our lifetime that takes the edge off our hopefulness, knowing we have less and less time ahead in which to be hopeful. Sometimes it seems as if we are going on not out of desire or joy but simply by force of habit, because it is simpler to continue than to change or stop. We may be happy enough. But are we really still alive, are we acting with as much heart as we are capable of? We probably don't know and don't have the energy, the interest, or the courage to ask. In our younger years we knew the sting of despair and anguish. These were terrible, of course, but at least we knew we were completely alive when we felt them. We don't want them back, but it may just be that in some ways our present condition is worse, or, at least, more insidious. Years, possibly decades go by while the suitors eat us out of house and home, but all the while we've been busy with other concerns and have not noticed—until, possibly, it is too late.

So, yes, we must finally recognize and admit that we stand at an important threshold; we can't avoid it any longer. We must recognize here that a battle is necessary to root the suitors out of our house once and for all, so that we can be ready to face with full creativity what is to come, and so that we will be able to love.

The Odyssey is rather dramatic and drastic in making this point, as I have just been. But we might just as well see this battle royal with our own deeply rooted inertia as something humorous or even silly. Zen usually takes a more lighthearted, even ridiculous approach to such things. In speaking about essentially the same point, Master Wuzu said, "It's like a water buffalo climbing through a window. The head, horns, and legs all pass through. Why can't the tail pass through?"

You see the picture here: a water buffalo is not standing on the threshold, he is stuck in it. Trying to pass through the window to get outside, the buffalo is hung up on the windowsill, unable to push through or pull back. A commentator on the story points out that if the buffalo squeezes through it will fall into a ditch below the window; if it squirms back it will be stuck inside forever. And oddly, though the big parts, the head, the horns, the legs, all pass through, the tiny little tail won't fit. Quite a predicament.

The water buffalo—the most common of all household animals in China and India, even today—symbolizes the mind or heart, that is, human consciousness, the seat of our spirituality, of our inner life. As I mentioned at the outset of this book, the process of spiritual awakening is often depicted in Zen as the taming of a water buffalo (often referred to as an ox). The basic outline of the taming process goes like this: searching for the ox; finding, taming, and riding the ox; ox and rider disappear; and, finally, returning "to the world with gift-bestowing hands." We can equate all this more or less with the process we have been describing: going out, turning back toward home, struggling along the way with our desires and confusions, and, finally returning fully to our place at home, where we reveal ourselves to those we love. But before we can do this last bit, before, that is, Odysseus can reconcile with Penelope, there is one more thing to resolve. It seems apt to see this in terms of a drastic battle, but we could also see it as a matter of a little tail that must pass through.

What's that little tail? What is the great reluctance that lurks within us, preventing us from overcoming our inertia and really loving? Remember, we're now at Ithaca, standing at the threshold of our own home. This means we've already come quite a distance. We know ourselves pretty well. We've confronted our desire, our ambivalence, our egotism, and a host of other gross defects that had been tripping us up for years. We haven't overcome them all, but at least we are aware of them and their nature and are therefore less subject to being sunk by them when life's next little wave rolls over us. In a sense, we have done all the really tough work. We've taken care as best we could of our noticeable, most telling defects. What's left is small, yet most difficult exactly because it is small; it will require great strength to overcome. This last difficulty is deeply—even fiercely—rooted, which is why a battle is required. In Buddhism this little tail is often called "clinging to a self," the last bit that needs to fall away before we can enjoy our full awakening.

Here we come to the bottom of the pervasive nature of fear. Our deep-seated basic fear is rooted in the very mechanism of our sense of identity. Who do we think we are? The body, the thoughts, feelings, desires, cherished viewpoints, relationships—all this is us. But we know this is all pretty shaky stuff. The body ages and dies. Thoughts come and go and are boring or unreliable most of the time. Feelings are also unreliable and often unsatisfactory; the ones we like we can't produce at will, and even when they do come they pass away quickly. Our viewpoints are mostly unexamined—it's debatable whether we actually believe them anyway—and our relationships are as apt to drive us crazy as make us happy. In other words, our identity is inherently dubious, entirely unstable, and false. At the deepest levels of our psyche we know this and it terrifies us. And when the time comes for us to reveal and give ourselves in love, we feel it—or avoid feeling it by telling ourselves and our lover a deceptive tale.

As we find in *The Odyssey,* and as we will find in our own lives, the only way out of this dilemma is through it. We have to admit who we are, accept our shakiness, vulnerability, and falseness, and reach out from there. There is a profound realization in this. Recall the story of my Zen friend who had been afraid for thirty years before he discovered that he didn't need to pretend he wasn't that way anymore, that he could be afraid and could ask for help. "Please help me," he'd say out loud or silently if someone else was around. "Please help me." And even though he didn't know who he was calling out to, it helped him. Later on it enabled him to reach out to me, another flesh-and-blood person.

When we are finally ready after long travail to admit to our fear, and let go of all our strategies of avoidance, our anger, distraction, or despair, we can learn to ask for help. I would call this humility: admitting who we are without shame or pride, we can—and we must—finally turn toward another in love.

Let's practice with this: Settle your body and mind where you are sitting. Breathe in and out with enjoyment, with awareness, with release. Let whatever is inside you be there; be aware of it with gentle curiosity but be willing to let it go to make room for whatever else wants to come. Continue to stay present with the breath and the feeling of the body as you do this.

Now, in this calm and peaceful state, consider deeply the Four Truths of Buddhism. First, all conditioned existence is suffering.

Conditioned existence is suffering not because life is so terrible, but because life is temporary: every moment passes, everything we are or have passes. We now know this is true. We know it as life's nature. It's the place where we began, and the place to end. The threshold. We accept and take joy in life as it is, not as we had hoped it would be. Breathe now and reflect on this.

With the second truth we understand the cause of our suffering: it is ourselves, our fear, our clinging to identity. Wanting to be someone, to do something, unwilling to accept the contingent nature of our lives and selves, we held on foolishly to illusions. It was this holding on that made us suffer. Standing here and now at the threshold of our lives we admit this to ourselves. Breathe now and reflect on this.

The third truth comes to us as an enormous relief, a joyous, easeful exhalation: We walk through the doorway; suffering comes to an end. At this point in our lives we have nothing more to prove. At last we are capable of letting go of all we've wanted and feared. Letting go with every exhalation. Again and again.

The fourth truth is that the homecoming journey is the way, the path to peace and the end of suffering. All we have suffered through, all we have been practicing, has served us in good stead. It has not been easy but it is all right. Breathe and reflect peacefully on this.

Now our hearts are full. What else is there for us but to offer our life to others? What else remains but love?

With the suitors and their allies gone, and the halls cleansed with fire and brimstone, you'd think that all has been done and that peace is at hand. How many times along our journey have we imagined this to be the case and found that it wasn't? Yes, we are close. But there's no final destination until life's last breath. For as long as we move and breathe, our victories are not final. As long as consciousness illuminates the body there will be further surprises, deeper challenges. The suitors may be dead, no longer to menace our household. But killing, even metaphorical killing, doesn't bring final peace. Odysseus knows that killing invites vengeance, and that he must brace himself for a further onslaught. The allies, fathers, and other kin of the suitors are sure to raise an army and descend quickly upon his household. As always, however, Odysseus has a plan. He directs everyone to say nothing of what has happened within the palace walls. Instead they are to make preparations for a gala wedding feast, so that all will believe Penelope has chosen one of the suitors for her husband and celebrations are in order. This will buy them time for further scheming. With all this in motion, Odysseus sets off to the country to see his father, Laertes. Reconciliation with him is the necessary next step.

21 / Laertes, or Forgiveness

There are many kinds of meetings. Some are pleasant, some are not; some are fulfilling, and some are inconclusive. In its own way, each is challenging. Each meeting changes us utterly as we proceed on our journey. We prepare for these meetings in our dreams or reflections, in times of repose, or work, or contemplation; but when the time comes to confront another, whether in love or enmity, much is required of us, and we never know what will happen. We can be ready, but we can never be fully prepared. The meeting of Odysseus and Laertes represents yet another facet of the bright gem of possible and necessary human meetings. Again the meeting is between father and son, younger and older person, but this time the father is in despair and grief at the end of his life, and the son needs to help the father as much as to be helped by him.

As we've heard throughout the poem, Laertes, since the death of his wife, Anticlea, and the long absence of Odysseus, has withdrawn from normal life. This is why Penelope has been weaving his shroud: all Ithaca expects him to die soon. He lives far from town, on his rural estate, where he tends to his vineyards, gardens, and olive groves. In winter he sleeps with the slaves by the fire; in summer he lies outdoors on scattered leaves. He entertains no visitors, dresses in ragged servant's attire, and comports himself in silence. When he hears that his grandson Telemachus has set sail in the middle of the night for Pylos, his response is to refuse all food and drink. He appears to be waiting and wishing for the death that will end his grief and misery.

In all the other cases in which Odysseus withheld his identity from family members there was a clear reason: he was scheming to defeat the suitors and couldn't risk being discovered until he was ready. Now as he prepares to meet Laertes, however, such strategic considerations do not apply. The suitors have already been dispatched and Laertes is completely isolated from Ithacan society. Odysseus realizes all this. When he first sees the sad figure of his father clad in rough leggings and a goatskin cap he agonizes over how to approach him.

> *Torn, mulling it over, this seemed better:*
> *test the old man first,*
> *reproach him with words that cut him to the core.*[1]

This is odd. Why does Odysseus feel the need to act with such seeming cruelty? Why not simply throw his arms around his long-lost dad? But this is not what he does. Odysseus begins by insulting Laertes for his appearance and apparent lack of energy and decorum. He then weaves yet another false biographical tale, telling Laertes he hails from "Roamer-Town . . . My father's Unsparing, son of old King Pain, and my name's Man of Strife . . ." These odd names evoke both his own and Laertes' suffering. His detailed story builds to Man of Strife's fictitious meeting with the great Odysseus, at whose mention the old man claws the ground, flinging dirt over himself in a wild paroxysm of grief.

This, apparently, is the point to which Odysseus wanted to drive him. The sight of his father so thoroughly in the grip of his anguish cuts through Odysseus' heart and he reveals himself at last. Like Telemachus and Penelope, Laertes is at first wary; he needs proof that it really is Odysseus and not an imposter or god who faces him. Odysseus reveals his scar, and, more, identifies the trees Laertes had planted for him as a child: thirteen pear, ten apple, forty fig, and vineyards: the very vineyards in which father and son now stand. Hearing all this, "Laertes' knees went slack and his heart surrendered." He threw his arms around his son and nearly fainted with joy.

Why Odysseus feels the need to go through this obscure process with Laertes, however happily it ends, has puzzled many commentators on *The Odyssey*. What can we make of it for our purposes?

I once saw a woman on a morning television show who had worked out a method for achieving happiness that had to do with writing in a journal for about twenty minutes every day. In this practice, you were to write about several different areas of personal concern—physical (including diet and exercise), emotional (how often you were angry or sad), relationships (how you spoke to and felt about your loved ones), and spirituality (your feelings about God and the inner life)—and use the writing to keep track of yourself. Under the category of spirituality she included forgiveness as a regular daily topic of meditation and advised that, every day, you write in your journal about your efforts to forgive yourself for what you had done that was harmful, and to forgive others for what they might have done to you.

I was startled by what this practice implied: that there is so much hurting going on routinely every day that every person needs to spend some daily time in active forgiveness practice. I had never considered that. But it is probably true that hurt occurs every day—all sorts of insult, abuse, hostility, disrespect, and diminishment. We suffer explicit hurting in anger, violence, deprivation, oppression, but also the more subtle hurting that comes from failing to love enough, failing to acknowledge and appreciate oneself and others, the kind of hurting that goes almost entirely unnoticed in families and workplaces and yet is actually a powerful negative factor in our lives. So it would make sense that taking good care of yourself would involve the hygienic discipline of forgiveness.

Yet very few people take up the practice of forgiveness, because it is unpleasant and difficult. You can't forgive without confronting pain, which no one likes to do. When we feel hurt we want to avoid the pain, so we reflexively look for a way out. If possible, we simply ignore the hurt. Or we distract ourselves from it in whatever way we can. If that doesn't work, we look for someone to blame. Blame—even if it is entirely justified!—is a form of distraction from our suffering. It substitutes drama for pain. When I've got a good blaming story going I can occupy myself with the weaving of that false tale. I can elaborate on it and fret over it; I can share it endlessly with my friends, and this will keep me from allowing myself to actually feel my loss or my dishonor, my shame, or defeat—whatever sort of hurt I want to avoid. The tale-telling occupies all my creative and emotional energy, so I don't have to notice the wound I'm nursing. Instead of feeling hurt, which makes me seem like a victim, now I can feel antipathy, indignation, anger—which makes me feel like a warrior.

Forgiving begins with the sober moment when I am willing to see the truth about my blaming story and allow myself to feel my suffering and know that it is mine; it does not belong to the person who has, in my blaming tale, "made me" suffer. I have to recognize that I have been using the blaming tale to avoid myself, to build up self-righteous resentment or self-justified despair. I have to let the blaming tale go and feel my suffering. When I do that honestly and thoroughly enough, I will naturally notice the pain of the other. I will see that the action that hurt me so much was really the consequence of his or her own pain, and the confusion that came of it. When I feel that, I can forgive. I become capable of saying to the other person, "It's not your fault, you did the only thing you knew how to do." The person may still be responsible for reaping the consequences of his or her actions; but my own heart is unburdened of its tale of grief and woe. My forgiveness will heal me, and it may also afford some comfort and healing to the other as well.

In *The Odyssey* Laertes is wrapped up in his own self-inflicted blaming tale. He's convinced that his fate is woeful, his life useless, the world is going downhill, there's nothing to be hopeful about, nothing to live for. This sounds convincing (just read the newspapers!) but it's never true. The world has forever been in terrible, even dire shape and people have always lost people they value and love. True, Laertes lost his wife and needs to grieve. But he hasn't lost his son, though he's convinced himself that he has. Now he's gone beyond grief: he's obsessed with his imagined losses; he's woven into them an elaborate story of defeat to justify his despair. This is why Odysseus can't be straightforward in revealing himself to Laertes. He must precede revelation with the painful process of insult and false story that will cut through Laertes' blaming tale and bring him to his senses. What must it have been like for Laertes to be seared yet again and most acutely by the absence of the son he loves so well—and to be so seared by words that come from the lips of that very son, who stands before him! Something in Laertes must have known who was speaking to him, just as something in him was unwilling to know. Breaking through his false story by hearing another false story told by Odysseus brought him to crisis—and then to joy.

The practice of forgiveness is deep and necessary. We must come to terms with it now, at this crucial threshold moment. We think of forgiveness as a part of the social sphere, which is true, but forgiveness is also a basic spiritual practice, with ever-deepening dimensions. If you practice meditation or prayer regularly, you know that it is sometimes not so peaceful or so comforting. In the openness of heart that true meditation or prayer fosters, sometimes our resentful or callused heart comes directly into view, and we can't deny it.

As we've just discussed, the pain in our hearts can arise in relation to a hurt we've suffered at the hands of another. But it can also come when we have caused others—or ourselves—pain, for which we need to forgive ourselves. We are all imperfect; this is our nature. Even though we are limited creatures in a limited world, we have an unlimited capacity to imagine goodness as well as to judge and criticize, and we inherently bear resentment against the selves we cling to. We might do battle with this clinging at the threshold, but we never defeat it entirely. So, regardless of how good or bad any of us may be, we all must forgive ourselves simply for being who and what we are. Just as we come in the end to forgive another for what he or she has done to us, so in the end do we need to come to the place—a place that we can only reach through the pathway of our own tears—where we can utterly forgive ourselves; where we can say to ourselves, as we might say to another, "It's not your fault, you are the only person you could have been."

In the end, we all require this deep forgiveness. Because it really isn't our fault. Our pain is ultimately caused neither by ourselves nor by others: it is simply built into our nature, into life's nature. Because we are living, feeling human beings in a difficult world, we have pain in our hearts, regardless of what happens or doesn't happen. To practice ultimate forgiveness you have to feel this pain all the way to its core. You've been hurt, it's true. Someone has done this to you or you have done it to yourself. But the ultimate cause of the hurt isn't self or other; these are only incidental causes. Hurt is a built-in condition of being alive. If you can get to that level of experiencing the pain of having been hurt (or of having hurt another, which is really the same thing: victim and oppressor are always locked in the embrace of pain; they require each other), then forgiving follows naturally because you see that we are all in this together. Knowing this, we can forgive another person, we can forgive ourselves, we can forgive the world, we can forgive God. Forgiving, we are forgiven. As John of the Cross writes in *The Living Flame of Love,* "Great is the wound, because He is great Who has wrought it; and great is the delight of it: for the fire of love is infinite."[2]

Let's practice forgiveness now. Begin with the basic mind-fulness practice that we have been cultivating throughout this book: settle with the feeling of the body sitting, then with the breathing, gradually coming to quiet, to full presence, simply, without restriction or constriction. Open up space inside, allowing whatever wants to be there simply to arise. In this way, come to readiness for the practice of forgiveness.

Now recall an incident (it need not be major, it could be something quite small) in which you or someone else acted with a degree of thoughtlessness or even cruelty. Paint a picture of this incident in your mind. Remember as best you can the place, the circumstances, the words, the gestures. Let the moment float there in your mind's eye.

Now go deeper with your feelings about the incident. However minor it may have seemed at the time (and may actually have been, in the grand scale of things), let yourself be perhaps more sensitive than you ought to be: feel the pain in you caused by the slight (if it is something you have said or done, feel the shame or regret). Explore this painful feeling, not overdoing it, yet allowing yourself to be vulnerable enough to feel it completely.

Now, based on this feeling, think, "This is not only my pain, it is *the* pain. This is the pain we all feel when we have been dishonored, diminished, dismissed. Due to this pain and its deep unconscious roots in me (or him or her), those words or deeds arose. Now I understand. Understanding, I can forgive. I am responsible, he or she is responsible, for actions of word or deed. Forgiveness does not take away that responsibility. And yet forgiveness changes me. It brings me closer to homecoming."

Work for a while actively forgiving, in this spirit.

Then rest in the feeling of forgiveness. See what thoughts or feelings arise in your heart, now that forgiveness is there.

And now, in the middle of this resting place, feel yourself surrounded by love, a deep and forgiving love that takes all into account, accepting everything, the good with the bad, the painful with the pleasant. Beyond any hurt, beyond any deed, this big forgiveness pervades all. You can breathe in and out with it, drink it in, suffuse it throughout the cosmos. "All is forgiven, all is redeemed, the power of love is infinite." Feel the quiet power of these phrases.

Odysseus defeated the suitors with the help of Telemachus and his faithful retainers. Having achieved that victory, he was capable of reconciling with Penelope. He is now about to face his final challenge: to defeat the suitors' avengers. To take this on, Odysseus needs Laertes, whom he must meet in full and ultimate forgiveness. Laertes, in fact, will deliver the decisive blow that brings the hostilities finally to a close, so that all can enjoy the peace so long desired.

22 / Peace

Eventually, the fathers and friends of the suitors discover what has really happened in the palace. After recovering the bodies, they work themselves into a fury for revenge and rush to Laertes' estate for the attack. There they are met by Odysseus, Laertes, and loyal retainers, as well as Athena-Mentor, who has already petitioned Zeus, king of the gods, to end the fighting once and for all.

Nevertheless, the two armies clash. Laertes, made magnificently noble and strong by Athena's magic and the forgiveness that has cleansed his heart, kills the opposing ringleader, which begins the general combat. But before anyone else can be slain, Athena stops them: "Hold back, you men of Ithaca, back from brutal war! / Break off—shed no more blood—make peace at once!"[1] All lay down their arms, and Athena delivers peace pacts that will keep the kingdom free of violence for years to come. Thus, at last, tranquillity and true homecoming are achieved, and our poem ends on this happy note.

What does peace mean to us, at this juncture in our travels?

Throughout this book I've been telling stories of people with whom I've practiced Zen over a lifetime. I am not so young anymore and neither are many of them. As we go on together, and the years roll by, we begin to realize that the time of coming home, coming all the way home to utter and complete peace—to death, the ultimate completion of life's journey—is at hand. Not that I or my friends are planning to die soon, or that we are shutting down our businesses or careers and saying good-bye to our spouses and children. But we are recognizing that, if the spiritual practice of a lifetime means anything at all, it must mean that when the time comes (and we feel it now much more personally than before), we must be ready to turn toward death, and see this not as a tragedy or a failure but rather as a homecoming, a return, the culmination of all we've been and done, rather than the scuttling of it.

In Buddhist thought, old age and death are seen as one thing, described with a single term. And, in the chain of karma, the root cause of old-age-and-death is birth, life itself. All this acknowledges that hurt is truly built into life. Life ripens into aging and death. This is life's destiny, its destination, life's true home. The journey there is not easy, of course, but it is fruitful. It is possible that the process of aging and dying is the richest and deepest of life's unfoldings, and that the challenge of our lives is to realize this. Our contemporary world does not much appreciate it. Youth is considered best; age is to be avoided and even overcome with gene-splicing or some as yet undiscovered miracle drug. Death is not even to be discussed. For the foreseeable future, however, aging and death will be with us, so we might as well make use of them. One of their beautiful features is that we all share in them equally. King or beggar, sage or fool, we all age and die, and in this we are all exactly alike, whatever our surface differences. Maybe if we appreciated this we would be more sympathetic to one another.

The time comes in every life when we are like Odysseus at the end of *The Odyssey*: still very much alive and vital, we've come completely home at last, embraced our loved ones, and settled our affairs. While we hope we'll live for many years to come, we've received and acknowledged the prediction of our death. This hasn't dismayed or depressed us. Far from it: we take comfort in it. Knowing we're going to die—and we know it because we've seen parents, spouses, loved ones die; we've been there with them and we know it's real—we are settled in our lives and appreciate them. The trials and tribulations of our youth are behind us now. We aren't bitten as deeply as we were by the sharp teeth of desire and obsession. Life for us now is more heartfelt, more peaceful, more grateful.

On the glorious long night of Odysseus and Penelope's reunion, Odysseus shared with Penelope what Tiresias had told him in the Land of the Dead. More than a prediction, Tiresias' words were instructions to Odysseus on how to approach his death:

> The prophet said
> that I must rove through towns on towns of men,
> that I must carry a well-planed oar until
> I come to a people who know nothing of the sea,
> whose food is never seasoned with salt, strangers all
> to ships with their crimson prows and long slim oars,
> wings that make ships fly. And here is my sign,
> he told me, clear, so clear I cannot miss it,
> and I will share it with you now . . .
> When another traveler falls in with me and calls
> that weight across my shoulder a fan to winnow grain,
> then, he told me, I must plant my oar in the earth,
> and sacrifice fine beasts to the lord god of the sea,
> Poseidon—a ram, a bull and a ramping wild boar—
> then journey home and render noble offerings up
> to the deathless gods who rule the vaulting skies,
> to all the gods in order.[2]

Tiresias is telling Odysseus that, to prepare for his death, he must go roaming yet again through many towns and cities where he can appreciate the range of human life. He must carry with him on these travels an oar, which stands for the seafaring or journeying that has been the chief characteristic of his life's story, as it has been of ours. And in these travels he is to look for a land and a people who know nothing of seafaring, have never seen a boat, don't even know what an oar is—and that's how he will know them. When they see the heavy oar slung across his shoulders they will think it is a winnowing fan, a tool for separating grain from chaff.

So Odysseus is to go forth one last time to find the place beyond all journeying, a place so rooted and so stable in its peacefulness that the very idea of journeying is foreign to it. And there he is to plant his oar as if it were a tree, and make special sacrifices of gratitude to the gods. From there he is to return to Ithaca where he again must make sacrifices. After all this he will be ready to let go of his life.

The other day a friend of mine, who is a hospice worker, said to me, "My work is making me realize that I've got to prepare for my own death. Can you help me understand how to do that?" What could I say to him? I've never died (at least as far as I can remember), and so can't know what death is. If I don't know what death is, how can I know how to prepare for it? Earlier, I told the story of the Zen master who, when a desperate student asked about the difference between life and death said, "I won't say!" I think what he really meant was "No one can say!" but he phrased it the way he did so that he did not cut off his student's questioning mind with too definite an answer. The student needed that desperate questioning not so that he could find an answer to what death is, but so he could appreciate and live his life. For, as we've amply seen by now, every life unfolds in the shadow of death, and the only way to live fully and truly is to recognize this.

Every one of us is like that student; we can't help but have a deep question about life and death. That's human consciousness: we are the creatures who speak and imagine; we are therefore the creatures who know we're going to die, and who can fear something we call "death." But it may be that there's no such thing as "death." What we call death may be a projection of our minds that covers the fact that we can have no idea what happens to us at the end of life—what we don't and can't know (especially when it is the most salient fact of our existence!) we fill with our fearfulness. The paradox of death is that it is happening not only at the end of life but at every moment of life; no fresh moment can arise without the death of the previous moment. And yet, if we look for death, try to seize on it, define it, analyze it, know or experience it in any way, we can't do it. By its very nature, death remains elusive to the living. Though it is thanks to death that life goes on, death can never be known. In this sense, death doesn't exist. So it's not death we fear. We fear the unknowable, the inconceivable. We can't conceive of it, can't imagine it, can't get at it in any way, and yet we know it is inescapable, so it terrifies us. The trouble is that in fearing what we call death, we also necessarily fear life.

It seems then that we've come to yet another, perhaps the deepest, seat of our human fear. At this dark place within us, as so many philosophers and sages have pointed out, we carry our dread of what we call death. It is the source of all our anxiety, all our trouble and unhappiness. It is also the source of all our accomplishment, all our creativity. Why do we so desperately seek love and constantly fear we won't get it or, having gotten it, fear we will lose it? Because we die and we don't know what death is, and we hope love will save us. Why do we constantly grasp for something, some reputation, some position, some wealth, some security, and never feel we're getting it, and when we do get it, worry that we'll lose it? Because we die, and we don't know what death is and hope that what we have or are will save us. Why are we driven to grope for meaning, to create monuments, religions, works of art, citadels of thought and language? Because we die and we don't know what death is and we feel compelled to know and to create works that will transcend death.

The Talmud has a wonderful story to this effect. Rabbi Yochanan was known as a great expert on death. He had seen many sages and ordinary people through the passageway from this world to the next, and so when his time came the rabbis all pleaded with him to send word back to them from beyond the grave, so that they would finally know what lay on the other side. Rabbi Yochanan agreed to do this. After he died he appeared to one of the rabbis in a vision and gave him his impression of dying. "It was quite easy and pleasant," he told the rabbi. "As simple and painless as removing a hair from a bowl of milk. But here's the surprising part," he went on. "As soon as this happened I felt a such a tremendous relief and release that I realized with a start that all my life, without my ever recognizing it I was so inured to it, I'd had a tremendous anxiety about dying. It had been with me from my first breath to my last—till now."

So my answer to the hospice worker who asked me how to prepare for death was, "There is no way. Don't even try. Instead try to live, to let go of every moment of your life so you can appreciate the moment that is just now coming. If you can live with that kind of renunciation then I think you can die." I also told him that, in my opinion, hospice work is falsely defined as "caring for the dying." No one is ever "dying," at least any more than anyone else. We are all of us, at all times, one breath away from dying, and in the meanwhile, whether we are six years old, or ninety-six and bedridden in our final illness, we are all alive, completely alive. So hospice work is about living, appreciating living, at life's most crucial and poignant moments. If we do hospice work, or care for a dying friend or relative, we can know this, just as we can know it very well if we ourselves are on our death bed, or even if we simply reach that certain age—Odysseus' present age—when we know for sure that we will die, and that this is more than just an idea. Of course we always knew it—everyone always knows it. But now we *really* know it.

Zen masters are famous for writing poems on their deathbeds. You can find whole books of them, translated now into English. The Zen masters of our contemporary American Zen community have also said some memorable last words. When priest Issan, who had been a female impersonator and a San Francisco show business phenomenon before his ordination, was on his deathbed, a close disciple said to him, quite emotionally, "I will miss you." "Why? Are you going somewhere?" Issan replied. Another of our old Zen adepts was a tea master. He'd studied for some years in Japan and practiced tea at the teahouse we have at Green Gulch Farm Zen Center. In tea it is polite to say, in Japanese, before you drink the first bowl of tea, *"Osakini,"* which means, "Please forgive me for going first." When he was on his deathbed, the tea master asked one of the people attending him to lean in closer. *"Osakini,"* he said to her, just before he breathed his last.

A few years ago I was able to spend a good deal of time with another of our Zen friends who was nearing the end of her life. She'd studied Zen for many years, but her main practice had been motherhood. A single mother, she'd raised her son well, and now, as she was dying, he was with her almost every day. Seeing the genuineness of his love, she felt confident of his goodness and strength as a person, which made her feel that her spiritual path was complete: she knew she'd loved her son well, that he'd been able to receive that love, and that was all that mattered; the rest was just fancy decoration, robes, and incense. Since she was dying near the Zen Center she had plenty of visitors. "People come to comfort me," she told me once. "But I think they're really coming to comfort themselves, so I let them. They're afraid, but I'm not. Death isn't scary at all! I'm ready to shove off into the big, dark sea." I wasn't with her when her life ended, but I am told it ended with a deep peacefulness.

The Rambam, the great medieval Talmudist, perhaps the greatest rabbi in all of history, thought that death was essentially the final leg of the journey home. In his treatise on repentance, he taught that the greatest repentance was death itself. For the person who, at the moment of death, will turn his or her life toward God, all will be forgiven, the Rambam said. In this case, far from being a tragedy and a miserable fearful comeuppance, death is life's fullest and deepest blessing.

In classical Buddhism the meditation on death is considered the greatest of all meditations, for more than anything else it wakes us up to the preciousness and seriousness of our lives. We have already practiced one form of this meditation (p. 137) when we made our initial visit to the Land of the Dead. The Buddha's last words echo this precious reminder: Life is short, impermanence is swift. Work out your salvation with care! Santideva, too, constantly brings us back to the recollection of death as a primary motivating factor for our lives:

> *The wanton Lord of Death we can't predict,*
> *And life's tasks done or still to do we cannot stay,*
> *And whether ill or well, we cannot trust*
> *Our lives, our fleeting momentary lives.*[3]

On the other hand, it is possible to get too carried away with the drastic specialness of death, forgetting that death (whatever it is) has always been our best friend, since it has been with us constantly, in between all the moments of our life. In this sense, death is not such an unusual or important thing. One great Tibetan lama used to say that we should not worry about death, because "Nothing happens." This seems, quite obviously, true. And there is the wonderful story of Zen Master Dongshan, who shaved, put on his robe, struck the bell, and announced his impending death to the assembled monks. Sitting in formal meditation pose he began to perish right before their eyes. The monks began to wail and lament, and continued to do so for some time, until finally the master recovered himself, opened his eyes, and said, "You should know better than this! People struggle to live and make much of dying. But what's the use of crying?" Seeing that his words did nothing to assuage the grief of the monks, Dongshan got up from his seat and went to work with them preparing a wonderful feast that was to take place after his demise, expecting that this would cheer them up. But after seven days, their tears still flowing, he gave up on them. "You monks have made a great commotion over nothing. When you see me pass away this time don't make a noisy fuss." And he retired to his room, sat down, and died.[4]

Indeed, there is nothing to make a fuss over. Nothing at all.

·   ·   ·

Still, there's no denying that the idea of death moves us, and moves us more the older we get. In ancient India, from the Buddha's time to the present, this was well understood. Then, as now, people who had raised a family and established a livelihood often saw the last part of their lives as a time to devote to spiritual pursuits, so that they could deepen their appreciation of what life is and has been as death comes closer. A contemporary Western version of this understanding is slowly beginning to dawn. More people are now conceiving the last part of life not as a time for pleasant "retirement," but, in a sense, the opposite of this. Now people in their late fifties, sixties, and older, still strong and quite able, are finding that, rather than a retirement, they want to make an advancement into a new life. This new life is not a life of outward journeying, but rather a last, poignant search for the place beyond all journeying: a place where an oar is no longer used for strenuous paddling but instead for winnowing—separating the wheat of a lifetime from the chaff. In that place you plant your oar rather than row with it, and you make sacrifices of gratitude to the gods for all that you've been given in your lifetime. And you continue to live out that settled appreciation, giving what gifts you have to give, until life's thread has completely unwound, and the story of your journey on the stormy sea is at last complete.

Or is it? Buddhism has two entirely opposite views of what happens after a life well lived. Theravada Buddhism preserves the original concept of Nirvana, or cessation: that at the end of the life of a perfect sage nothing else happens, just total and utter peace. The long, restless round of desire and transmigration ended, the sage is gone, utterly gone, all trials and tribulations at an end. Mahayana Buddhism proposes the opposite: that great sages do not enter Nirvana and will not enter it until all the world's suffering beings are saved. Instead, they are born again and again into this world, but not in pain and thirst, like the rest of us, but out of love, and in response to their great vow to save all sentient beings from harm, without exception.

At the funeral for Ayya Khema, a great Western Buddhist nun, this funny opposition was played out. I was conducting the funeral in partnership with Achaan Amaro, a close friend of mine who is, like Ayya, an ordained Theravadin monastic. After we performed all the requisite ritual acts, Amaro and I both stood to offer words. Amaro spoke of the limitless peace of cessation and complete release Ayya was now able to enjoy—or not to enjoy, because she was now blessedly and utterly gone at last, a condition to which she had been aspiring all her life. I then rose and thanked Ayya for her great compassion in being willing to return again and again to continue to teach us not only throughout our lifetimes, but in lifetimes to come.

In my mind, these funeral orations were not dueling doctrinal statements but rather complementary visions, two sides of a coin that represents one of the many attempts we poor living humans have made to describe how we feel about the human journey, and its final return home, that is so inconceivable to us.

Here are Odysseus' words, as he shares with Penelope Tiresias' final prediction for him:

> *And at last my own death will steal upon me . . .*
> *A gentle painless death, far from the sea it comes*
> *to take me down, borne down with the years in ripe old age*
> *with all my people here in blessed peace around me.*
> *All this, the prophet said, will come to pass.*[5]

Odysseus' death is not a good death, an honorable glorious death, like Achilles', nor is it, like Agamemnon's, a death of disgrace and failure. Odysseus' death is just death, plain and simple, as gentle and painless as lifting a hair from a bowl of milk or plucking a spent blossom from a cherry tree. He moves on, far from the sea, with those he loves beside him, though they cannot accompany him. His ability to surrender to this final destination comes as a result and culmination of all he's lived through and felt, of his great determination, his surpassing wiliness, his endurance, loyalty, and faith.

May we too be ready to surrender when the time comes, not only at the end of our lives, but on every moment of our lives. For every moment is and has always been, at its perfect center, a déjà vu moment: timeless, peaceful, inconceivable. Every moment has been far from the sea, even when we were on the sea at its stormiest. It has taken us long years and many dramatic adventures to discover this, and maybe we never have discovered it, instead continuing to struggle our whole life through with our Cyclopes and our Lotus Eaters, with our Scyllas and Charybdises. But if that's so, it's what we've had to do. For if nothing else, we've learned that there is no concept, there is no template, there is no model for a life deeply lived. The sea of stories rolls on and on without end. Though we must tell and listen to our stories well, trying as much as we can to understand, we know now that there's a peace beyond understanding, a love too boundless to be known, a tale too secret to be told.

As long as space endures
As long as there are beings to be found
May I continue likewise to remain
To drive away the sorrows of the world

Notes

Book Epigraphs

1. George Lakoff and Mark Johnson, *Metaphors We Live By* (Chicago: University of Chicago Press, 1980), p. 239.
2. Steve Benson, *Open Clothes* (Berkeley, Calif.: Atelos, 2005), p. 24.

PART ONE: SETTING FORTH

Epigraph

1. Homer, *The Odyssey*, trans. Richmond Lattimore (New York: HarperCollins, 1976), Book 2, p. 49, line 388.

1: The Sea of Stories

1. *The Odyssey*, trans. Richard Fagles (New York: Viking, 1997), Book 1, p. 77, lines 1–6.
2. Simone Weil, *Waiting for God* (New York: Putnam), p. 129.

3: Waiting

1. Weil, *Waiting for God*, pp. 112–13.
2. Isaiah 40:31.

4: Speak Your Grief

1. *Odyssey*, trans. Fagles, Book 2, pp. 94–95, lines 43–52.

5: False Stories

1. *Odyssey*, trans. Fagles, Book 1, p. 79, lines 72-75.
2. *Odyssey*, trans. Fagles, Book 1, p. 87, lines 336–42.

6: Leaving Home

1. *The Odyssey,* trans. Robert Fitzgerald (Garden City: NY: Doubleday & Co., 1961), p. 39.
2. *Odyssey,* trans. Fitzgerald, p. 21.
3. Simone Weil, *Gravity and Grace* (Lincoln: NE: Bison Books, University of Nebraska Press, 1997), pp. 162–63.
4. Shantideva, *The Way of the Bodhisattva,* trans. Padmakara Translation Group (Boston: Shambhala, 1997), p. 162.

PART TWO: DISASTER

Epigraph

1. *Odyssey,* trans. Lattimore, Book 11, p. 171, lines 110–11.

9: Working with Disaster, Pleasure, and Time

1. *Odyssey,* trans. Lattimore, Book 5, p. 94, lines 219–24.
2. *Purity of Heart and Contemplation,* ed. Bruno Barnhart and Joseph Wong (New York: Continuum, 2001), p. 166.
3. Abraham Joshua Heschel, *Between God and Man,* ed. Rabbi Fritz Rothschild (New York: Free Press, 1997), p. 229.

10: The Lotus Eaters: Remembering to Practice

1. *Odyssey,* trans. Fitzgerald, pp. 95–96.
2. Paraphrased from *Odyssey,* trans. Fitzgerald, p. 208.

11: Being Nobody

1. Emily Dickinson, *The Complete Poems of Emily Dickinson,* ed. Thomas H. Johnson (Boston: Little, Brown & Co., 1960), p. 133.
2. *Odyssey,* trans. Lattimore, Book 9, p. 151, lines 534–35.

12: Fatigue

1. *Odyssey,* trans. Lattimore, Book 10, p. 154, lines 78–79.

13: Circe, or Desire

1. *Odyssey,* trans. Fagles, Book 10, p. 237, line 260.
2. *Odyssey,* trans. Fagles, Book 10, p. 239, line 301.

14: The Land of the Dead

1. *Odyssey,* trans. Fagles, Book 10, p. 246, lines 547–48.

16: Impossible Choices: Scylla and Charybdis

1. *Odyssey,* trans. Lattimore, Book 12, p. 192, lines 258–59.
2. Weil, *Waiting for God,* p. 166.
3. Martha Nussbaum, *Upheavals of Thought: The Intelligence of Emotions* (New York: Cambridge University Press, 2001).

PART THREE: RETURN

Epigraph

1. *Odyssey,* trans. Fagles, Book 22, p. 451, line 414.

17: Sleep

1. Thomas Merton, *Inner Experience* (New York: HarperOne, 2001), p. 138.
2. *The Blue Cliff record,* trans. Thomas Cleary and J. C. Cleary (Boston: Shambhala, 1992), p. 10.
3. *Dogen Zenji, Shobogenzo,* vol. 2, trans. Kosen Nishiyama and John Stevens (Tokyo: Nakayama Shobo, 1997), p. 153.
4. *Odyssey,* trans. Fagles, Book 19, p. 408, lines 631–38.
5. *Odyssey,* trans. Fagles, Book 13, p. 296, lines 331–34.

18: Reveal Yourself!

1. *Odyssey,* trans. Fagles, Book 16, p. 345, lines 244–49.

19: Love's Risk

1. Martin Buber, *I and Thou,* trans. Walter Kaufman (New York: Charles Scribner's Sons, 1970), pp. 54–55.
2. *Odyssey,* trans. Lattimore, Book 23, p. 339, lines 66–67.
3. *Odyssey,* trans. Fagles, Book 23, p. 465, lines 342–43.
4. *Odyssey,* trans. Fagles, Book 23, p. 465, lines 342–43.

20: On the Threshold

1. *Odyssey,* trans. Fagles, Book 22, p. 440, lines 37–42.
2. *Odyssey,* trans. Fagles, Book 22, p. 454, lines 342–43.

21: Laertes, or Forgiveness

1. *Odyssey,* trans. Fagles, Book 23, p. 475, lines 264–66.
2. St. John of the Cross, *The Dark Night of the Soul and The Living Flame of Love,* trans. Robert Van De Weyer (New York: HarperCollins, 1995), p. 182.

22: Peace

1. *Odyssey,* trans. Fagles, Book 24, p. 485, lines 584–85.
2. *Odyssey,* trans. Fagles, Book 23, p. 464, lines 304–20.
3. Shantideva, *The Way of the Bodhisattva,* p. 42.
4. *The Record of Tung-shan,* trans. William Powell (Honolulu: University of Hawaii Press, 1976), p. 68.
5. *Odyssey,* trans. Fagles, Book 23, p. 464, lines 321–25.

Bibliography

Buber, Martin. *I and Thou*. Translated by Walter Kaufman. New York: Charles Scribner's Sons, 1970.

Lakoff, George, and Mark Johnson. *Metaphors We Live By*. Chicago: University of Chicago Press, 1980.

Merton, Thomas. *Inner Experience: Notes on Contemplation*. Edited by William H. Shannon. New York: HarperOne, 2003.

Rothschild, F. A. *Between God and Man*. New York: Free Press, 1951.

St. John of the Cross. *The Dark Night of the Soul and The Living Flame of Love*. Translated by Robert Van De Weyer. New York: HarperCollins, 1995.

Shantideva. *The Way of the Bodhisattva*. Translated by the Padmakara Translation Group. Boston: Shambhala, 1997.

Weil, Simone. *Waiting for God*. Translated by Emma Craufurd. New York: G. P. Putnam's Sons, 1951.

Weil, Simone. *Gravity and Grace*. Translated by Arthur Wills. New York: Putnam, 1952.

Welty, Eudora. *One Writer's Beginnings*. Cambridge, MA: Harvard University Press, 1983.

About the Author

Norman Fischer is a poet, author, Zen priest, and abbot. Founder and teacher of the Everyday Zen Foundation (www.everydayzen .org), he is one of the senior Zen teachers in America. In addition to his own retreats and events, which take place in his groups in Canada and Mexico, as well as the United States, Norman teaches at many other meditation centers around the world. His approach to meditation is known for its flexibility and openness. Norman also regularly works with businesspeople, lawyers, Jewish meditators, conflict resolution specialists, and others to share the spirit and practice of Zen beyond the formal trappings. He has taught at Harvard, Yale, Brown, and Stanford universities.

Fischer has been publishing in Buddhist magazines for many years, and is on the advisory board of *BuddhaDharma* magazine. His essays have been anthologized many times, and have been included in every annual edition of *Best Buddhist Writing* (Shambhala). Among his spiritual books are *Opening to You: Zen-Inspired Translations of the Psalms* (Putnam, 2002) and *Taking Our Places: The Buddhist Path to Truly Growing Up* (HarperSF, 2003), which was on the *San Francisco Chronicle* bestseller list. A graduate of the Iowa Writers' Workshop, Norman has been associated with the lively San Francisco Bay Area literary scene since the 1970s. The most recent of his dozen collections of poetry are *Slowly but Dearly* (Chax Press, 2003) and *I Was Blown Back* (Singing Horse Press, 2005). He lives with his wife, Kathie, in Muir Beach, California, near Green Gulch Farm Zen Center, where he served as abbot until 2000.